Aunt Susie's
10-MINUTE
BIBLE RECIPES

Aunt Susie's
10-MINUTE
BIBLE RECIPES

Bringing God Into Your Life One Dish At a Time

· SUSIE SIEGFRIED ·

FAIR WINDS
PRESS
GLOUCESTER, MASSACHUSETTS

First published in the USA in 2003 by
Fair Winds Press
33 Commercial Street
Gloucester, MA 01930

Library of Congress Cataloging-in-Publication Data available

ISBN 1-59233-026-6

10 9 8 7 6 5 4 3 2 1

Cover design by Patricia Fabricant
Illustration by Ed Parker
Book design by Laura Herrmann Design

Printed and bound in Canada

DEDICATION

———◦∾∾◦———

*To my niece Paula, who had the confidence
to give me a try as a writer,
and to my daughter Stacey, who has assisted
me in so many ways. Thank you so much.*

TABLE OF CONTENTS

—⁕—

FOREWORD

—⟡—

*L*ove of God, love of family and friends, love of life, and love of good food are the mainstays in this wonderful world that God has created for us. Love and food are synonymous to me, as are God and love. My mother spent hours making the foods we loved—handmade noodles, homemade devils food cake, "made from scratch" peach dumplings—because she loved us. My sisters and I continued that tradition in our homes, sharing our love of God and our love of good food with friends and family, and building a lifetime of happy memories along the way.

I called upon those happy memories in the writing of this book. Each recipe is inspired by a verse from the Bible, and accompanied by a story which reflects the theme of the Scripture. The recipes are ones that I have gathered over the years—recipes that have been passed down through family, recipes from friends and neighbors, as well as many that I have created myself. All are 10-minute recipes, in that they require work time of 10 minutes or less, but cooking time will vary. In some of the recipes you will find Aunt Susie's Tips, little tidbits of information here and there to offer some helpful advice.

With God's love, love of family and friends, and good food to share with each other, how can we not be grateful for a blessed life? Thank you, God, for your gift of nourishment both for our bodies and our souls.

APPETIZERS, SOUPS & DIPS

*...and when I saw her, I wondered
with great admiration.*

REVELATION 17:6

*L*ois lost her husband very early in life. He was forty-nine years old when he died. They had three children at the time, one of whom still lived at home. Their youngest son was eleven years old, pretty young to lose a dad. She sorely missed her husband, but with God at her side, encouraging her when she needed it, she carried on with determination and a lot of spunk. She retired when she was seventy, after waking up many a morning at five o'clock to be at work by six or seven in the morning. She worked hard to give her son a good home and be a mom he could be proud of. I've never heard her complain or be bitter about life's tough blows. Lois is now in her early seventies, is in good health, and is enjoying her grandchildren as well as her children. Like Esther, she is admired, respected, and looked upon in favor by those who know her. She is a proud, independent woman of faith, and I am proud to call her my sister and my friend.

The admiration of others is something we earn by our behavior. This is truly a blessing, and it is helpful to know that God is only a prayer away.

TACO DIP

Moms and kids alike will admire this delicious dip.

SERVES 8 TO 10

2 cans refried beans

2 avocados, mashed

1 cup (230 grams) sour cream

¼ cup (60 grams) mayonnaise

1 package taco seasoning

1 cup (180 grams) chopped tomatoes

1 bunch green onions, chopped

1 3-ounce (85-gram) can sliced black olives, drained

1 8-ounce (225-gram) package of finely shredded cheese

DIRECTIONS: Spread refried beans on large plate or pizza pan, and then spread the avocado over beans. Mix sour cream, mayonnaise, and taco seasoning together, and spread over the avocado mixture. Sprinkle the shredded cheese on top of that. Scatter your tomatoes, olives, and onions in a pretty pattern so it looks appealing. Serve with any kind of tortilla chips or Doritos. Very quick appetizer.

aunt susie's tips:
You can refrigerate this and serve later. You may also heat this in the microwave and serve warm.

And to knowledge temperance;
and to temperance patience;
and to patience godliness.

2 PETER 1:6

*W*hen I think of patience, I always think of my father. Named Joseph after the father of Jesus, he was the epitome of patience. One day, Dad was balancing the checkbook and came in and said to Mom, "Margaret, you've overdrawn the account again." And Mom looked at him, smiled, and said sweetly, "Oh, no, Joe. You just underdeposited." With that, he looked at her, grinned, turned around, and went back to his office to finish his task. Would that the rest of us could react so well. I'm reminded of the saying that we shouldn't take life so seriously; it's not permanent.

God's patience is without limits. The next time you feel impatient, count to 10 and reflect on his patience with you.

CHILE CON QUESO

Your patience won't be tested with this recipe,
as it is so quick and easy.

SERVES 4 TO 6

1 pound (455 grams) Velveeta cheese, cut into chunks

1 small can tomatoes and green chilies

¼ teaspoon minced garlic

½ tablespoon chopped onion

DIRECTIONS: Put all ingredients into fondue pot. Heat and stir until melted. Serve with any kind of chips that are good to dip.

aunt susie's tips:
May also be cooked in the microwave on medium power or over the stove on medium heat.

Make haste to help me, O Lord my salvation.

PSALM 38:22

lmost everyone has done it—I've done it more than once. You get out of the car and lock it automatically, only to realize a second too late that you've locked your keys in the car. One day I did it again, but this time I really did it. My six-month-old granddaughter was still in the car, belted in her car seat. The worst part was that she was too young to know how to unlock the door. Luckily, it was a nice day and the weather wasn't bad, so I didn't have to worry about her freezing or suffocating due to the heat. She was asleep when it happened, which was very lucky for me, as that gave me time to use my neighbor's phone to call for help. And, need I say, I was also calling on God, as usual, for His aid once more. As I waited for help, my little one woke up. Peering in at her through the window, I desperately tried to entertain her until help arrived, making silly faces and noises and playing peek-a-boo—whatever I could think of to make it seem like a game to her and to keep her from becoming upset. She was awake for only about five or ten minutes before the police came to my rescue—and hers.

I cannot begin to count how many times God has sent someone to help me when I needed it. Be ready to help others when God calls on you.

Sweet Cheese Appetizers

Even when you think you don't have time to help out, you
can whip up this appetizer and take it to a friend.

Serves 10

1 10-ounce (280 grams) jar pepper jelly
1 8-ounce (230 grams) package cream cheese, softened
Crackers

DIRECTIONS: Pour jelly as desired over softened cream cheese. Serve
with crackers.

aunt susie's tips:
*I like to warm the jelly in the
microwave for about 10-20 seconds.
These are delicious with
Triscuit crackers.*

Beware of false prophets...
Ye shall know them by their fruits.
Do men gather grapes of thorns or figs of thistles?

MATTHEW 7:15

*E*very once in a while, we hear about people alleging to have seen UFOs and even claims of being abducted by aliens. A long time ago when I was in my thirties, I drove a forty-mile paper route in the early morning from about four to six o'clock, when it was still dark outside. One particular morning I had been driving for a few miles when I noticed something strange in the early-morning sky. I couldn't make out the shape very well, but something about it was making me feel nervous and scared. It seemed to follow me wherever I went. Racing through my route in record time, I finally finished, nervously praying all the way home. As I neared my home, I heard on the radio that there had been some kind of accident in the East, and the gases formed a strange yellow-gray formation in the eastern sky. Thanking God for His protection, I sighed with relief but felt so foolish at the same time for letting my imagination get the best of me.

Whenever you find yourself in a fearful situation, remember that God is right there with you.

GRAPE CHILI MEATBALLS

This three-ingredient recipe may sound scary,
but it's surprisingly tasty!

MAKES 60 MEATBALLS

2 18-ounce (510-gram) packages frozen meatballs
1 10-ounce (280-gram) jar grape jelly
1 12-ounce (355-milliliter) bottle chili sauce

DIRECTIONS: Put meatballs into large pan on top of the stove. Pour grape jelly and chili sauce on top and stir. Heat at medium. Let heat through. Ready in about 10 minutes, if thawed.

aunt susie's tips:
*For a different meatball glaze,
try 1 cup (230 grams) of
peach preserves, 2 tablespoons
of horseradish sauce, and
1 teaspoon of dry mustard.*

And now abideth faith, hope, charity, these three;
but the greatest of these is charity.

1 CORINTHIANS 13:13

When my husband, Larry, was in the Navy, the Navy assigned him to Norfolk, Virginia, in 1970. We rented a house in Norfolk and met some of the nicest, charitable, and most generous people I've ever known. Being far from home with no relatives around can be very difficult, especially when your husband is out to sea for weeks and even months at a time, but we found some wonderful friends down the street. Bernard and Marie and their son, Darwin, a teenager at the time, became more than friends to our children and to us. Darwin was a great sitter, and Bernard and Marie became pseudo-grandparents to our children. These nice folks opened their home and their hearts to us. I think God sent these special angels into our lives, and what angels they were. Many a time we spent the night with them when Larry was out to sea and we were lonely or scared. They helped us make those times more enjoyable and less difficult, and we will never forget them. I hope that we have been as helpful and as full of charity to our friends when they needed it.

Don't take for granted the wonderful friends God has placed in your lives. Keep passing on the favors you have received.

CHEESY ONION DIP

Pass along this easy-to-make dip
the next time you get together with friends.

SERVES 8

3 cups (480 grams) chopped Vidalia onions

2 cups (226 grams) shredded Monterey Jack cheese

1 cup (110 grams) shredded Swiss cheese

2 ½ cups (590 grams) mayonnaise

Garlic powder to taste

DIRECTIONS: In a large bowl mix all ingredients together. Bake in a greased 9" baking dish at 350°F (180°C) for 35–40 minutes. Serve with any kind of chips.

My friend Kathi shared this recipe with me.

Thou therefore endure hardness,
as a good soldier of Jesus Christ.

2 TIMOTHY 2:3

My first attempt at being a do-it-yourself woman came when I was a naval wife in Norfolk, Virginia. My husband, Larry, was assigned to one of the ships at the naval base, and he was out to sea quite a bit. It was really hard having to do everything alone. Larry was out to sea when the faucet in the bathroom would not turn off. It just kept running and running no matter what I did. I tried to reach the landlord, but to no avail. I had no idea what to do. I ran to my neighbor's home three doors down. Since he was knee-deep in a project of his own, he decided to give me help—one step at a time. First, he told me how to shut off the water with the shutoff valves under the sink. Then, he proceeded to the next step, and I would run home, try to do it, and then run back to him for the next step. In some cases, I would have to go back for more detailed instructions and try again. A few hours later, after many trips to my neighbor's and a trip to the hardware store, my faucet was fixed. Success! We, as a nation, take for granted the hardships that our military men and women and their families endure.

We usually appreciate our soldiers only in times of crisis. Take the time to pray for our military members and their families in times of peace as well as war.

Artichoke Dip

This all-American dip is very popular with military families around the world; make some for a friend serving our country as a thank-you.

Serves 10

2 14-ounce (400-gram) cans artichoke hearts

1 6-ounce (170-gram) package shredded Parmesan cheese

³/₄ cup (180 grams) mayonnaise

Garlic powder to taste

¹/₂ teaspoon lemon juice

Dash hot sauce, optional

Paprika to garnish

DIRECTIONS: Drain and chop artichoke hearts into small pieces. Mix well with all other ingredients. Place into a greased 10" × 10" casserole dish. Bake for about 35 minutes at 350°F (180°C) until crispy around the edges. Sprinkle paprika on top and serve on Triscuits or taco chips.

My sister-in-law Gayle shared this recipe with me.

> *Favour is deceitful, and beauty is vain:*
> *but a woman that feareth the LORD,*
> *she shall be praised.*

PROVERBS 31:30

I remember pouting as a child when I didn't get my way, and my sisters would say, "Your face is going to freeze like that." Then I would get just a little bit nervous and worried that they might be right, so I changed my expression. Of course, I always wanted to look pretty and have a nice smile, as did most girls. I remember Mom saying, "Pretty is as pretty does." She would always emphasize that being a good person with a kind word for others and a positive attitude was one of the most important things in life, and that was what made you beautiful. Today there is so much more emphasis placed on physical beauty—a well-toned physique and youthful appearance. Where is the emphasis on the beauty within? Magazines, television, the Internet, and movies inundate us with images of physically beautiful people, beautiful by today's standards.

This makes teaching our children about the importance of inner beauty an even more difficult task. People's true beauty is on the inside. The rest of it will fade away.

Take the time to look around, and you will discover the beauty of God in those around you.

CORNED BEEF & SAUERKRAUT

This may not look pretty—but try it and you'll
appreciate its mouth-watering taste.

SERVES 8

4 ounces (115 grams) corned
beef, cut up

1 15-ounce (425-gram) can
Bavarian sauerkraut, drained well

4 ounces (115 grams) Swiss cheese

4 ounces (115 grams) Monterey
Jack cheese

1 cup (235 grams) mayonnaise

1 tablespoon horseradish

Dash salt

Dash pepper

DIRECTIONS: Mix all ingredients and place into a greased 8" × 8"
baking dish. Bake for 30 minutes at 350°F (180°C). Serve with crackers.

My friend and neighbor Maryann shared this recipe with me.

*Receive him therefore in the
Lord with all gladness . . .*

PHILIPPIANS 2:29

When my husband, Larry, worked for the federal government, we had the wonderful opportunity to meet people from countries all over the world. Larry taught some international courses to foreign students, some of whom were coming to the United States for the first time. Since we were some of the first Americans they would be meeting, we wanted to be sure to make them feel welcome. One of the most interesting visitors we welcomed was a gentleman named Mohamed from Djibouti, a country between Somalia and Ethiopia. He intrigued all of us with the story of his harrowing rescue of his mother-in-law and sisters-in-law from Somalia. Since they were in much danger in Somalia, he traveled by night and brought them through many areas of gunfire on a dangerous journey back to his home in Djibouti. They now live safely with him, his wife, and their three children. What a wonderful experience it was for our children to hear about how difficult life was for this man and his family. It helped our children to appreciate how fortunate they are to be living in the United States.

We're always welcome in God's home. Make someone feel welcome in your home this week.

Apricot Wings

A great way to welcome a neighbor or a friend, new or old.

Makes 20 Wings

4 tablespoons margarine

Approximately 20 chicken wings, cut up

³⁄₄ cup (240 grams) apricot preserves

¹⁄₄ cup (85 grams) honey

1 teaspoon beef soup base

1 teaspoon minced onion

DIRECTIONS: Preheat oven to 425°F (220°C). Melt margarine in a 9" × 13" pan. Flour chicken wings. (Fill a plastic bag with flour, put in a few wings, and shake the bag.) Place floured wings in pan. Bake for approximately 45 minutes to 1 hour, turning wings over halfway through. Combine apricot preserves, honey, beef soup base, and minced onion. Brush onto chicken wings after cooked and bake for an additional 5–10 minutes.

aunt susie's tips:
I warm up the apricot preserves and honey mixture in the microwave so it spreads easily and is not so thick.

And Jesus came and touched them . . .

MATTHEW 17:7

I love to give hugs, receive hugs, send hugs by e-mail, and receive hugs by e-mail. I get such a good feeling from sending and receiving hugs. It is such a simple act, but it can be so powerful. A hug can say so many things. In sad times, it can say, "I'm here for you. I'm so sorry for you." It can also say, "I love you. I care for you." It can help heal our pain. It can say, "I'm thinking of you." It can help warm up a cold day. A few years ago, I went into the license bureau for my yearly license plate renewal. Standing in line a few steps ahead of me was a tall gentleman wearing a round button that said, "I love hugs." Well, now, I love hugs, too! Without thinking (I'm good at that), I went up to this man and said, "Hi," and, to his surprise, I gave him a hug and said, "I love hugs, too!" He was a little startled, and then we both started laughing. Then, as everyone else standing in line at the license bureau realized that I didn't know this gentleman, they started laughing along with us.

Send a hug, give a hug, but do it today. Thank you, God, for hugs.

SPINACH BALLS

Take these to a friend—along with a big hug, of course.

MAKES ABOUT 30 BALLS

1 10-ounce (285-gram) package frozen spinach, thawed

1 6-ounce (170-gram) box chicken-flavored stuffing

3 eggs, beaten

1/2 cup (120 grams) mayonnaise

1/2 cup (75 grams) shredded Parmesan cheese

2 teaspoons minced onion

6 tablespoons butter or margarine, melted

DIRECTIONS: Mix all ingredients and drop by spoonfuls onto a greased cookie sheet. Bake at 350°F (180°C) for 10 minutes.

My friend June shared this recipe with me.

...And there was very great gladness.

NEHEMIAH 8:17

Grandma Siegfried developed some eccentric behaviors in her late seventies. One was to ride the bus all day long. Soon the bus company was very annoyed and called to complain that she was riding all day long but paying only one fare. They seemed to think they were losing money. So my dad and his sisters and brothers bought her a pass for the bus. She then rode the bus every day for hours and thoroughly enjoyed it. On holidays and special occasions, we had to go downtown to the courthouse square and wait for the buses so we could try to find Grandma and bring her home for celebrations. She was fortunate that we lived in a small town and in the time that we did so that she had the freedom to enjoy life in her own way. She rode the bus until she became ill, and we brought her home with us. What a simple thing it was for her to enjoy. Would that we could all do that same kind of thing in our own lives.

Open your eyes and your heart to enjoy the simple pleasures of life. God has surrounded us with them.

Asian Vegetable Soup

Gladden the heart of an elderly friend or relative
with this nutritious, delicious soup.

SERVES 6

8 cups (1.9 liters) canned chicken
broth, or chicken-flavored soup
base added to water

1 large package Asian vegetables

1 8-ounce (225-gram) can sliced
water chestnuts, drained, optional

$1/2$ teaspoon garlic powder

$1/2$ teaspoon onion powder

DIRECTIONS: Bring chicken broth to a boil. Add Asian vegetables and cook as directed on package. Add water chestnuts, garlic powder, and onion powder; stir well.

aunt susie's tips:

I use chicken soup base instead of canned chicken broth because I think it gives it a much better flavor and more of a homemade taste.

...and healed them that had need of healing.

LUKE 9:11

*W*hen Ed was in his late thirties, he went to the doctor because he wasn't feeling very well. The doctor ordered some preliminary tests, and soon after, he was admitted to the hospital for further testing. The test showed that he had leukemia. He was then sent to a larger hospital out of town, where more treatment was available for him. Ed was active in his church back home, and hundreds of prayers were being sent to heaven for his recovery. Church members, friends, relatives, and even people who had never even met him prayed for him. After his treatment in the hospital, he underwent chemotherapy. It was such a wake-up call, not only for him, but also for his family and friends. Today he enjoys good health and is thankful to the Lord for his healing and for the many prayers of so many caring people. Not to mention the chicken soup his mother made for him.

Pray for all those who need healing in their lives—and remember, cooking for someone is an active form of prayer.

CHICKEN VEGETABLE SOUP

Make this soup for an ailing friend.
The healing power of chicken soup is legendary.

SERVES 6

8 cups (1.9 liters) chicken broth

1 package frozen vegetables
for stew

¹/₂ cup (90 grams) quick-cooking
barley

¹/₄ teaspoon garlic powder

¹/₄ teaspoon onion powder

1 cup (140 grams) cooked chicken
breasts, cut into bite-sized pieces
or shredded

DIRECTIONS: Bring chicken broth to a boil. Add frozen vegetables and barley. Add seasoning after cooking vegetables and barley for 10 minutes. Add chicken and cook an additional 10 minutes. Add more seasoning if desired.

aunt susie's tips:
*I always add extra seasonings about
10 minutes before serving the soup.
It gives it a good flavor.*

The troubles of my heart are enlarged:
O bring thou me out of my distresses.

PSALM 25:17

*B*eing new parents is a time filled with much joy, worry, and distress. Only a few days after we brought our new son home, we had to take him to the doctor for his congestion. The doctor told us to buy a vaporizer. We went out and bought one right away and put it to use that very night. We set it up in our son's bedroom and hoped it would help. The next morning my husband woke me up and pulled me over to the mirror. His nose was all black. I said to him, "Oh, my gosh, what happened to your nose?" He replied, "It must be that vaporizer. We'd better check the baby." We rushed into the nursery, relieved to find that our son was fine. Still wondering what had happened, I walked into the kitchen and was shocked to see a pan with fire blazing out of it and a hole in its bottom. It seems I had forgotten about the nipples I was sterilizing at three in the morning and had gone back to bed and fallen asleep. There was soot all over the apartment— everywhere except the baby's room. Fortunately, we had closed the door the night before to let the humidifier do its work. Talk about a blessing in disguise. Had it not been for the congestion that led to the humidifier, which caused us to close the door, who knows how the baby would have reacted to the soot and fumes.

Don't be so busy worrying that you miss out on the present. Let God take over some of your worries—He's always there for you.

Asian Spinach Soup

Plan your week with meals like this easy soup, and you won't have to worry about what you're going to fix for dinner.

Serves 6

8 cups (1.9 liters) chicken broth

¹/₂ cup (55 grams) shredded carrots

¹/₄ teaspoon ginger

¹/₂ 8-ounce (225-gram) package rice sticks

1 cup (200 grams) precooked shrimp

1 cup (30 grams) spinach leaves

¹/₄ cup (25 grams) chopped green onions

DIRECTIONS: Bring broth to a boil in large pot. Add carrots and ginger. Simmer for 15 minutes. Add rice sticks, shrimp, spinach leaves, and green onions, simmering for 4 more minutes.

*But when they saw him walking upon the sea,
they supposed it had been a spirit,
and cried out…*

MARK 6:49

*L*ittle did I know when I married Larry back in 1966 that I was marrying a man who could walk on water, or wade through deep water anyway. Larry and I took our children and our nephew on a canoe trip. The kids were around eight and ten years old at the time. We took some soda pop along with us since we were going to be on a two-hour trip. While my oldest daughter, Stacey, Larry, and I were getting into our canoe, the boys got into their canoe and took off. They had a good head start, and we couldn't catch up with them. After paddling the canoe in the hot sun for a while, we became pretty thirsty, but the boys had all the pop in their canoe and were far ahead of us. We would yell at them at times when they were in sight, but, of course, they "couldn't hear us." They were having a great time sending empty cans down the river every now and then. By the end of the canoe trip, we finally saw the boys and were catching up to them. Larry was pretty upset. All of a sudden, he jumped right out of the canoe and started after the boys. It was fairly shallow water where we were, so he was running in the water. The boys looked worried and hurriedly pulled to the shore and sprang from the canoe. The image of Larry jumping out of the canoe and walking on water still makes us laugh to this day.

Although we cannot walk on water, God gives us the confidence to do many things we think we can't do.

LENTIL CHILI

You can warm up friends and family
with this lentil chili after a long walk.

SERVES 8 TO 10

1 small onion, chopped

1–2 tablespoons butter or margarine

2 tablespoons flour

12 cups (2.9 liters) chicken broth

1 1-pound (455-gram) bag dry brown
lentils, rinsed and drained

1 cup (185 grams) brown rice
(uncooked)

2–4 cups (280–560 grams) cooked
and shredded chicken

1 10-ounce (285-gram) package
frozen carrots

1 tablespoon cumin

Dash of pepper

1 small can chopped tomatoes,
optional

Dash of celery salt

Dash of dried cilantro leaves

DIRECTIONS: In large pot, sauté onion in butter until tender. Stir in
flour until onion pieces are coated and flour has heated. Gradually add
chicken broth and bring to low boil. Add lentils and brown rice. Let
simmer for 20 minutes. Add carrots, cumin, pepper, and tomatoes, if
desired. Add shredded chicken and continue to cook on medium to low
heat until carrots and brown rice are tender. Season with celery salt and
cilantro to taste. Garnish with shredded cheese, salsa, or sour cream.

My friend and neighbor Mary shared this recipe with me.

Remember the days of old, consider the years of many generations: ask thy father, and he will show thee; thy elders, and they will tell thee.

DEUTERONOMY 32:7

*O*wning your own store has both advantages and disadvantages. It was so exciting when my partner, Barb, and I opened our gourmet popcorn store back in 1983. We started out in my basement, and then we moved to a little 400-square-foot store in our local area. We prepared gourmet popcorn and created new popcorn flavors and concoctions. After a while, we decided we needed more room and exposure, so we moved to a local strip mall. We expanded what we offered, including all kinds of candy, homemade baked goods, and catering. When I retired and closed the store in December 1993, it was a sad day but also a thankful one. How many nice people I had met and how much joy they had brought into my life. What an experience it was. I still run into many of our old customers, and they always tell me how much they loved our store. The store may be gone, but the good memories will last forever.

Thank you, God, for the wonderful gift we call memory—which allows us to relive the joys of the past and remember loved ones. A memory well remembered is a kind of prayer.

MASHED POTATO SOUP

This soup brings wonderful memories of my mom
and what a great cook she was. I hope you will enjoy
this soup and make memories with it, as I have.

SERVES 4 TO 6

2 20-ounce (610-gram) packages
   instant mashed potatoes,
   prepared according to package
   directions

1/2 stick (55 grams) margarine

1/4 teaspoon chicken soup base

1/4 cup (40 grams) minced onion

1/4 teaspoon pepper, optional

3 cups (710 milliliters) milk

DIRECTIONS: Heat mashed potatoes in microwave for 40 seconds. Put
in pan and heat over medium heat. Add 1/2 stick of margarine, chicken
soup base, minced onion, and pepper. Gradually add 3 cups of milk using
whisk. Heat until warm enough to serve.

aunt susie's tips:

*I adapted this recipe from my
mom's original mashed potato soup.
You can top this with shredded
cheese and/or bacon pieces if desired.*

He maketh the storm a calm, so that the
waves thereof are still.

PSALM 107:29

*S*taying calm in stressful situations can be hard. But sometimes it
is essential. My daughter Stacey was driving my van one day, as
her car was in the shop. She was around nineteen at the time. I forgot
to tell her that I had a large fire extinguisher lying in the back of the
van. I had taken it to get recharged and had forgotten to take it out
of the van. As she was turning a corner, all of a sudden she heard a
loud noise, and a white gaslike substance started filling up the van.
She quickly pulled over and hopped out of the van, not knowing what
was happening. A couple of cars stopped to see if they could help; they
thought the van was on fire, and she wasn't sure whether it was or not.
After the hissing stopped, they all figured out what had happened, and
she drove the van home. When I saw her, she was white all over and
looked like a ghost. I couldn't imagine what had happened. But Stacey,
surprisingly, kept very calm. (I know that God had to have had His
hand over her, as she becomes hysterical over the slightest thing.) It
took days to clean that van up and get the fumes out. Her calmness
prevailed and she was just fine.

*If you get overanxious and have difficulty in keeping calm, call on God to
help you. He calmed the sea; He can certainly calm you.*

CREAMY RICE SOUP

This rice soup is as soothing to the body as it is to the soul.

SERVES 4 TO 5

2 tablespoons butter or margarine

2 stalks celery, chopped

1/2 cup (55 grams) shredded carrots

1/2 cup (80 grams) chopped onion

3 tablespoons flour

1 teaspoon salt

1/4 teaspoon pepper

1 1/2 cups (250 grams) instant brown rice

1 cup (240 milliliters) water

1 10-ounce (285 milliliters) can chicken broth

1 cup (240 milliliters) half-and-half

DIRECTIONS: Melt butter in saucepan over medium heat. Sauté celery, carrots, and onion in butter until tender. Stir in flour, salt, and pepper. Stir in brown rice, water, and broth. Heat until boiling. Reduce heat. Cover and simmer for 15 minutes. Stir in half-and-half and heat until hot. Do not boil.

My friend Marie shared this recipe with me.

aunt susie's tips:
You can purchase the shredded carrots and chopped onions in the produce department at your local grocers.

*Remember his marvelous works that
he hath done, his wonders,
and the judgments of his mouth.*

1 CHRONICLES 16:12

*O*ne of the things my children have really missed is grandparents. Sadly enough, my parents both died when I was a teenager, so they weren't around for some of the most important and wonderful moments in my children's lives. I remember when I was in the first grade, and I walked to school every day. I always walked by my Grandma Siegfried's house. Some days I would go to her house for a snack after school, like this "Rivella" soup. She taught me how to play some card games. Canasta and euchre were some favorites, and oh, what fun we had! I always looked forward to spending time with her. We laughed a lot and enjoyed each other's company. Now I am blessed with a granddaughter who is now nine years old. I pick her up from school nearly every day, and she stays with me until her mother comes to pick her up after work. We play cards and I make her "Rivella" soup. I hope these memories will be with her long after I am gone.

*Think how often God makes time for you—and take the time you need
to build memories with those you love.*

Grandma's Chicken "Rivella" Soup

Adopt my grandmother's soup and pass it on in your own family.

Serves 4

—⁕—

1 26-ounce (765-milliliter) can
  chicken and rice soup

1 can water (use can from soup)

"RIVELLA":

1 egg

1 cup (125 grams) flour

Salt to taste

DIRECTIONS: Put soup and water in pan and bring to a boil. Put flour in a small bowl. Break egg into flour. Dip fork in flour and mix egg and flour together until crumbly. Drop "rivellas" into soup, separating them with a fork so that they don't clump together. Boil soup for 1 minute. Simmer for 5 minutes. Add salt to taste.

aunt susie's tips:

This recipe was my mom's version of my Grandma Siegfried's soup, and I always make it when I'm in a hurry. You can extend this by adding 1 cup of chicken broth.

Woe is me for my hurt! my wound is grievous...

JEREMIAH 10:19

Marilyn and I were chitchatting when we heard this hysterical screaming. It was my daughter Stacey. We ran outside and saw her lying on the ground. She and her brother had been standing up on the teeter-totter, and she had fallen off, hitting her nose on the handle as she came crashing down, and landing on her arm. She was actually very lucky. There was a nail protruding from the center of the handle, and she landed smack dab on the center, hitting her nose directly on the nail. One more inch to either side and she might have lost an eye. Marilyn ran and got a wet cloth, as Stacey's nose was bleeding pretty badly. We got in the car and drove to the little town where they had a hospital. After cleaning her up and X-raying her arm, they told us we had to go to a bigger facility where they had a plastic surgeon. They gave her something for the pain, and we drove to our children's hospital, nearly four hours away. After seventy-three stitches inside her nose and a cast on her broken arm, we went wearily home.

When your children hurt, you hurt; when we hurt, God hurts.

MEATBALL SOUP

Kids love this; make it for a child you know who is hurting.

SERVES 4 TO 6

—◦◦◦◦◦—

1/2 32-ounce (905-gram) package
  frozen meatballs

2 16-ounce (475-milliliter) cans
  stewed tomatoes

5 cups (1.2 liters) water

2 medium onions

2 medium carrots

2 stalks celery

1/2 cup (120 grams) ketchup

1/2 cup (75 grams) ditalini pasta

1 tablespoon beef soup base

1 teaspoon oregano

1 bay leaf

DIRECTIONS: Put all ingredients in a large pot. Bring to a boil, stirring occasionally. Reduce heat. Cover and simmer for 1 hour.

My friend Shar shared this recipe with me.

SALADS

What shall I render unto the LORD
for all his benefits toward me?

PSALM 116:12

My friends calling to say, "Hi, how are you doing?" and cheer up my day. My granddaughter coming over to our house excited to see me. My children calling and keeping in touch. Getting up in the morning in good health and being in a cheerful frame of mind. How much I take all of these things for granted. I very seldom stop to think that all of these are gifts—gifts from God sent to His children. I expect these things to happen and don't realize how blessed I am to be the recipient of these many gifts. In this busy, sometimes hectic, life, I don't take the time to meditate or reflect on my daily living or thank God for all of the good things that happen. I just take them for granted, and if they don't happen, I get very upset and disappointed with my life.

God has given me quite a few wake-up calls, however, that have made me realize what things are truly important. When my husband, Larry, had his heart attack, that really woke me up and made me get my priorities in order. Times of crises in our lives really do open our eyes to how blessed we are in so many ways.

Realize how blessed and fortunate you are. It's so very important to start your day out right—praise and give thanks to our magnificent Father.

CRANBERRY SALAD

I serve this for Thanksgiving dinner every year,
but it's great any time of the year.

SERVES 6

2 cups (480 milliliters) boiling water

1 6-ounce (170-gram) package cherry gelatin

1 10-ounce (285-gram) package frozen strawberries in syrup, partially thawed

1 16-ounce (450-gram) can whole cranberry sauce

1 8½-ounce (250-milliliter) can crushed pineapple in syrup

DIRECTIONS: Add 2 cups boiling water to cherry gelatin. Add the rest of the ingredients to the gelatin mixture. Refrigerate until set.

My sister-in-law Gayle shared this recipe with me.

aunt susie's tips:
We always serve this for our Thanksgiving dinner. Great with turkey, chicken, or pork.

For the LORD shall be thy confidence,
and shall keep thy foot from being taken.

PROVERBS 3:26

"Lois, hold my hand. Lois, hold my hand." Words from a baby sister to her big sister every night. We four girls shared one bedroom in our home. Luckily, it was a pretty good-sized bedroom. I shared the bed with my sister Lois, or I should say that Lois shared the bed with me. She was fourteen years older than me and had to put up with me as a bed partner. Seems I never slept by myself. I always had someone to sleep with until all the girls left home. Then I slept with my mom an awful lot. Every once in a while Lois will remind me of how I used to ask her to hold my hand. This always gave me such comfort and a good feeling of being safe and secure. I think of this at times when I'm holding my granddaughter's hand, when crossing the street or shopping in the mall. Holding her hand not only expresses my affection for her, but it also helps her feel safe and secure. As our children and grandchildren grow older and break away from this hand holding, they start to feel more independent and confident and self-sufficient—yet once in a while they will still hold our hand. And then, of course, as the process reverses and we get older and need a hand to hold to steady us, their hands become our security and safety.

Each of us needs to feel safe. Extend a hand to someone who needs it,
as God extends His hand to us any time of day or night.

BROCCOLI CAULIFLOWER SALAD

Serve this salad with confidence, as it is as nutritious as it is delicious.

SERVES 6 TO 8

DRESSING:

1 cup (235 grams) Miracle Whip salad dressing or mayonnaise

¹/₂ cup (100 grams) sugar

2 tablespoons vinegar

SALAD:

1 12-ounce (340-gram) package broccoli florets

1 12-ounce (340-gram) package cauliflower florets

1 medium red onion, chopped

¹/₂ cup (115 grams) real bacon pieces

¹/₄ cup (35 grams) cashew pieces

¹/₂ cup (75 grams) golden raisins

¹/₂ cup (75 grams) dried cranberries, optional

DIRECTIONS: Combine dressing ingredients in a large bowl. Add remaining salad ingredients to dressing mixture and mix well. Refrigerate until ready to serve.

My sister Anita shared this recipe with me.

aunt susie's tips:

You can buy precooked bacon in your meat department at your supermarket to cut down on prep time. You can also buy jars of real bacon pieces, and they are a little bit cheaper than the precooked bacon.

And thou shalt rejoice in thy feast…

DEUTERONOMY 16:14

Have you heard the song "Make Someone Happy"? Well, we wanted to make our sister Marilyn happy and surprise her for her sixty-fifth birthday. All of us, sisters and spouses, flew out to Nevada to surprise her. We had planned it with her husband, Paul, and her daughter Paula, who was flying in earlier. Marilyn knew that her daughter and one of her grandsons were coming, but she wasn't expecting us. We went to a restaurant, as planned, and we sat down. As soon as we saw her coming, we put our menus up to hide our faces. When the hostess guided her over to our table, we pulled down the menus and yelled "Surprise!"—and what a jolt it gave her! She was so elated. We stayed and visited for a few days and had a great time. We had made T-shirts with pictures of all of us four girls when we were little and also our recent pictures. What a change. We laughed a lot the whole time we were there. It was a Kodak moment; a happy time we all shared together. It reminded me that in trying to make someone else happy, we often make ourselves happy as well.

God always provides us with means for our happiness. Follow His example—do something nice to make someone else's day.

Mandarin Feast Salad

A sweet salad you lovingly share with friends and family.

SERVES 6 TO 8

—◈—

DRESSING:

1 cup (216 milliliters) salad oil

¼ cup (60 milliliters) cider vinegar

1 tablespoon minced onion

1 tablespoon celery seed

⅓ cup (70 grams) sugar

1 teaspoon dry mustard

½ tablespoon paprika

SALAD:

1 1-pound (455-gram) bag mixed greens

¼ cup (30 grams) sliced onion

2 11-ounce (310-milliliter) cans mandarin oranges (drained)

DIRECTIONS: Mix dressing ingredients together. Serve with tossed greens, sliced onions, and mandarin oranges.

Be not forgetful to entertain strangers:
for thereby some have entertained angels unawares.

HEBREWS 13:2

*H*ospitality was a number-one priority back when I was co-owner of a gourmet popcorn store. Welcoming people, giving them samples of our delectable popcorn, and making them feel good was our goal. Naturally, when we went to the big city of New York for a food show where we had a booth to sell our product wholesale, this remained a number-one priority for us. It was very exciting. After the event, we took a bus back to our hotel. I still had some leftover samples of popcorn with me. First, I gave some to the bus driver, who was pleasantly surprised. Then, I began passing it out to my fellow passengers. What different reactions I received! Some people refused it completely; others were thrilled. One lady looked at me and said, "We can tell you're not from New York." Another person said, "Are you crazy?" But many people did accept it and tried it, and we began talking to one another. Many people got off the bus with a warm smile on their face, waving good-bye to us as they left.

God reminds us that strangers are just friends we haven't met yet. Go out of your way to befriend people you meet out in the world.

HOT AND CRUNCHY CHICKEN SALAD

This warm dish is an inviting entree for your next potluck dinner—a great way to meet new people.

SERVES 4

2 cups (280 grams) cooked chicken, cut into bite-sized pieces

1/2 cup (70 grams) cashew pieces

2 teaspoons minced onion

1/2 cup (60 grams) chopped celery

2 teaspoons lemon juice

1/2 teaspoon salt

1 cup (235 grams) mayonnaise

1/2–1 cup (60–120 grams) grated American cheese

1 cup (125 grams) crushed potato chips, optional

DIRECTIONS: Combine all ingredients except cheese and chips. Put in a greased 8" × 8" baking pan. Sprinkle with cheese. Bake at 400°F (200°C) for 15 minutes. Cover with chips and bake an additional 5 minutes.

My friend Jim shared this recipe with me.

And if he trespass against thee seven times in a day, and seven times in a day turn again to thee, saying, I repent; thou shalt forgive him.

LUKE 17:4

My children fought constantly while growing up. Now that they are grown, they get along much better, but they still fight amongst each other from time to time. I get so upset when they fight. I don't ever want anything to come between them. There are some times when they won't even speak to each other for a while, and it worries me so.

I hear of those stories where a rift has come between family members, and they never speak to each other again. When I hear about something like that, I always wonder what could have been of such significance to tear people apart and make them unable to forgive each other. So often, it is something small that grows and festers over time. My children have always been able to work out their differences. They tell me that they could never stay mad at each other for long; they care about each other too much to let anything come between them. What makes it so hard for some to forgive? It is such a small price to pay for such a grand prize—the love of a cherished family member or friend is priceless.

Our Lord constantly forgives us, almost minute by minute. Stop and forgive those you need to forgive. Don't wait any longer.

FRUIT SALAD

**Food is the perfect peace offering.
Let bygones be bygones with this fruit salad.**

SERVES 8

2 cups (460 grams) sour cream
2 teaspoons lemon juice
³/₄ cup (150 grams) sugar
¹/₄ cup (30 grams) powdered sugar
Pinch salt

1 8¹/₂-ounce (250-milliliter) can
  crushed pineapple, drained
¹/₂ cup (55 grams) maraschino
  cherries
¹/₄ cup (30 grams) chopped pecans
1 banana, sliced

DIRECTIONS: Blend together first five ingredients in a bowl. Stir in fruit and nuts. Pour into a 1-quart (.95 liter) mold or foil-lined muffin cups. Cover and freeze. Thaw at room temperature 10 to 15 minutes before serving.

My sister Lois shared this recipe with me.

For if they fall, the one will lift up his fellow:
but woe to him that is alone when he falleth;
for he hath not another to help him up.

ECCLESIASTES 4:10

*W*hen I first opened my catering and gourmet candy business in 1983, one of my main concerns was hiring people who would work for a small wage, but also work hard and be pleasant to all types of customers. Expected a lot, didn't I? I received much more than I ever hoped. I was fortunate to hire some terrific women who became my angels and dear friends. They gave me their all for very little compensation. I will never be able to repay them for their remarkable generosity and dear friendship.

When I became the sole proprietor of my store in 1988, I could not have done it without my friend Judy. She was my 'gal Friday,' and she ran the store for me for a couple of years. Judy could do anything and would do it well. When she left, I missed not only working with her, but also our close friendship. I still keep in touch with her and see her at least once a month as well. Shirley, Sharnell, and Kathi were my right arms until I closed the store in December 1993. Carol, Mary Ann, Marie, and June are just some of the many wonderful people that worked with me and have blessed my life. And I hope I am a better person because of them. It has now been a decade since I closed my store, and my friends and I are still taking care of each other's needs.

One of God's greatest gifts to us is the gift of real friends. Call or visit one of God's gifts today.

ALMOND CHICKEN SALAD

Almonds, a biblical favorite, make this salad special
enough for your favorite friends.

SERVES 8

DRESSING:

1 cup (235 grams) mayonnaise

³/₄ teaspoon curry powder

¹/₄ cup (50 grams) sugar

¹/₄ teaspoon ginger

1 tablespoon lime juice

¹/₄ cup (60 grams) Earl Grey chutney

SALAD:

1 cup (110 grams) slivered almonds

4 cups (560 grams) cooked chicken, cut into 1-inch pieces

¹/₂ cup (50 grams) green onions, chopped, optional

2 20-ounce (570-milliliter) cans pineapple chunks, drained well

¹/₂ cup (60 grams) chopped celery, optional

DIRECTIONS: Combine all dressing ingredients in a large mixing bowl. Mix well. Spray cooking sheet with nonstick cooking spray, and spread slivered almonds over it in a single layer. Bake at 350°F (180°C) for five minutes until almonds are golden. Add the cooked chicken, green onions, pineapple chunks, slivered almonds, and celery (if desired) to the mixture. Mix well. Refrigerate until time to serve.

aunt susie's tips:

I usually serve this with a gelatin sherbet salad and banana bread. It has a delicious flavor and is one of my favorites. Everyone loves this and always asks for more.

...And Esther obtained favour in the sight of all them that looked upon her.

ESTHER 2:15

*J*oelle loves all kinds of clothes and she wears them well. When she was about two and a half years old, she was anxious to have a new pair of Underoos underwear. She had seen them advertised on television. They had cartoon characters on them, and she was crazy about them. She wanted some very badly, but I couldn't find any at the stores in our area. One weekend our family went to visit my sister in Indiana, and we all went shopping at the mall. She took us to a particular store and showed Joelle the Underoos she had found, and bought a pair for her. Joelle was thrilled. Of course, she had to put them on right away. It was just too long to wait until we went home. With her new Underoos on, she was feeling great. As we walked through the mall, she would lift her dress once in a while to look at her new Underoos and say, "See how pretty?" We kept after her about lifting her dress, but she was just too excited. Everyone who saw her with her Underoos just grinned at this little girl who was so proud of her new clothes.

Children take such delight in the world God has created for us. Remember to see the world through a child's eyes.

SEVEN-LAYER SALAD

Even children who won't eat their veggies like
this easy-to-make seven-layer salad.

SERVES 8 TO 10

1 16-ounce (455-gram) package
lettuce

1 cup (200 grams) sliced water
chestnuts, drained

1 10-ounce (285-gram) bag frozen
peas, thawed

1 cup (160 grams) chopped onion

1/2 pound (225 grams) deli ham,
shredded

1 cup (115 grams) shredded cheddar
cheese

2 cups (470 grams) mayonnaise

1/4 cup (50 grams) sugar

DIRECTIONS: Evenly cover the bottom of a 9" × 13" pan with lettuce. Layer water chestnuts, frozen peas, onion, ham, and cheese. In a small bowl, combine mayonnaise and sugar and stir until smooth. Spread mayonnaise and sugar mixture over salad. Refrigerate until ready to serve.

And the LORD thy God will make thee plenteous in every work of thine hand…

DEUTERONOMY 30:9

My friend Barb was part of our prayer group, which met weekly. She and her family were enjoying a good life, with a nice home and a business she owned with her husband. Then her world fell apart, as they say. The business went bankrupt, and she and her husband lost their home and decided to divorce. At the same time, her youngest daughter moved out and into her own apartment. Her sixteen-year-old son moved with her to an apartment, and he was going through hard times as well. She was very worried that she wouldn't be able to find a job with which she could support herself and her family. We prayed in earnest that God would give her the confidence she needed to find a good job. The Lord answered our prayers as Barb found the perfect job. With His help, Barb turned her situation around and just recently bought a new home. I admire her so very much. In the face of adversity, she kept her faith strong and overcame her doubts about herself and her fears, and she became one successful woman. To this day, Barb holds dear the strength that God gave her to make things work out as well as the strength that God continually gives her.

God can give you the strength you ask for as well. Let go of the past and concentrate on the now and the future.

Spinach Salad

Spinach makes you strong—so here's a fantastic salad to strengthen you.

Serves 4 to 6

1 16-ounce (455-gram) bag spinach

1 cup (170 grams) sliced strawberries

½ cup (80 grams) cubed cantaloupe

½ cup (75 grams) dried cranberries

1 cup (150 grams) glazed walnuts, optional

DRESSING:

¼ cup (60 milliliters) plain yogurt

½ cup (120 milliliters) raspberry pecan salad dressing (Ken's Steakhouse is good)

2 teaspoons sugar

DIRECTIONS: Put spinach in bowl. Top with strawberries, cantaloupe, cranberries, and walnuts. Mix dressing. Toss dressing and salad all together when ready to serve.

aunt susie's tips:

Glazed walnuts and glazed pecans can be purchased at your local supermarket. I find this is too much dressing for my taste, so I toss half of the dressing with the salad and serve the rest on the side for those who like more.

...it was a chance that happened to us.

1 SAMUEL 6:9

W hen we started catering in our store, little did we know we would be catering for somebody famous. When we were called to cater a fund-raising event for one of our local legislatures, we were glad to have the opportunity to do so. Imagine our excitement when we found out that Barbara Bush would be there. I had to turn down people who wanted to help as there were so many who volunteered just for the chance to see Mrs. Bush. We were hoping to meet this powerful woman whom we so admired. We eagerly prepared our special chicken salad, flaky croissants, spinach salad, and praline brownies. We arrived early and prepared to serve the very large crowd. After serving everyone, we took a break and walked around the yard, hoping to see Mrs. Bush. This was an outside affair with tables in the yard, and Mrs. Bush was seated on the front porch. Since we couldn't get close enough to actually meet her, we decided that at least we could have our picture taken with her—with her in the background, that is. So we all huddled together about fifteen feet in front of the porch where Mrs. Bush sat, and one of the guests snapped our picture. There we all were, with Barbara Bush sitting on the porch behind us.

Many marvelous opportunities are presented to us by God; it's up to us whether or not we take advantage of them.

Chicken Pecan Salad

When the opportunity to impress someone special in your life presents itself, serve this simple yet sophisticated salad.

Serves 4

—◦◦◦—

3–4 chicken breasts, cooked and shredded

¾ cup (180 grams) mayonnaise

1 teaspoon poppy seed

1 teaspoon celery seed

⅓ cup (40 grams) chopped pecans

DIRECTIONS: In a medium bowl, combine chicken, mayonnaise, poppy seed, celery seed, and chopped pecans. Add more or less mayonnaise to taste. Refrigerate until ready to serve.

aunt susie's tips:
Grapes are a very good addition to this recipe. This is great served in a pita.

BEEF
DINNERS

O continue thy lovingkindness unto them that know thee; and thy righteousness to the upright in heart.

PSALM 36:10

Grandma had a beautiful vase that she had brought over from the Old Country when she immigrated to America. I always loved the vase. On one particular day, I picked up the vase and accidentally dropped it. It came crashing down to the ground and shattered into a thousand pieces. Tears welled up in my eyes, and I felt absolutely awful. I dreaded telling Grandma that I had broken her beloved vase. I'll never forget how understanding Grandma was when I told her. She told me that although the vase was precious to her, I was even more so. Those kind words are still with me today.

Acts of kindness beget more acts of kindness. How kind is our loving God! We need to emulate His kindness and treat others with the same loving ways He does us—His children.

SIMPLY MEATLOAF

Do an act of kindness today. Fix this meatloaf and take it to a shut-in or someone who is unable to cook for themselves.

SERVES 6 TO 8

2 eggs
⅓ cup (80 grams) ketchup
¾ cup (175 milliliters) warm water
1 envelope dry onion soup mix

1 cup (125 grams) soft bread crumbs (about 2½ slices)
1 cup (125 grams) crumbled crackers
2 pounds (910 grams) ground beef

DIRECTIONS: Beat eggs. Add ketchup, warm water, and soup mix to eggs. Add bread crumbs, crackers, and ground beef. Bake at 350°F (180°C) for 1 hour.

My sister-in-law Gayle shared this recipe with me.

Is it not to share your food with the hungry
and to provide the poor wanderer with shelter...

ISAIAH 58:7

*S*ome of us devote our lives to fulfilling this promise. Sister Dorothy is one of these people. She started a soup kitchen in Dayton called The House of Bread, which is still going strong today. She also started The Other Place, a day shelter for the homeless, and it is still ongoing. She has worked hard to help the poor locally and in third world countries. At nearly eighty, she is still working on projects to improve the lives of the many needy people in the area. God bless Sister Dorothy and all of those other wonderful people who work tirelessly to help the poor.

Let us honor the Sister Dorothys of the world and help them. Drop by your local shelter or soup kitchen today with a pan of this Rosemary Beef.

Hungry Wanderer's Rosemary Beef

This hearty meal is easily doubled or quadrupled to share with as many people as you might need to feed.

SERVES 8 TO 10

1 4–5-pound (1.8–2.3 kilograms) beef roast

2 tablespoons oil

1 1/2 cups (175 grams) sliced onion

1 teaspoon minced garlic (I use minced garlic from a jar)

1/2 cup (120 grams) ketchup

1 teaspoon dried rosemary

1/2 cup (120 milliliters) water

1/4 cup (60 milliliters) red wine vinegar

1 tablespoon Worcestershire sauce

1/2 cup (110 grams) brown sugar

2 tablespoons vegetable oil

DIRECTIONS: In large skillet over medium-high heat, brown meat in 2 tablespoons vegetable oil. Remove meat from pan. Sauté onion and garlic. In 5-quart (4.75-liter) pot or Dutch oven, combine remaining ingredients and sautéed onion and garlic. Place roast in pot. Cook slowly, covered, until meat is tender, about 3 hours.

My friend Sharon shared this recipe with me.

aunt susie's tips:
This can also be cooked in the Crock-Pot.
Adjust cooking time accordingly.

For I have given you an example,
that ye should do as I have done to you.

JOHN 13:15

Money makes the world go round, so they say, and it certainly can have a powerful effect on all of our lives, especially those of us who have a hard time making it financially. I remember a time when my young daughter and I went to a store to buy some things. The store was just about to close, and the lines were long. The total price of our items was $10.75. I handed the young woman running the register a $20 bill. She handed me back my change, and my daughter and I headed for the door. As I was putting my change away, I noticed that the young lady had given me back nearly $40. I realized that the cashier must have thought I gave her a $50 bill rather than the $20 that I gave her. I explained to the cashier what had happened, and sure enough, in her hurry to check all those people out quickly, she thought I had handed her a $50 bill. She thanked me for my honesty, and with that we left.

On the way out, my daughter asked me why I didn't just take the money. I asked her what she thought God would have wanted me to do. She replied without hesitation, "Give the money back." I told my daughter that whenever we are in doubt about what is the right thing to do, we should ask ourselves what God would want us to do.

We all know it takes courage for us to be honest. Do a mental check for yourself and start practicing the virtue of honesty in your daily life. God expects it.

Delicious French Dip

Bread and meat make an honest if homely meal. This roast takes some time to cook, but it is so, so simple and has a superb taste.

SERVES 6

—⟳—

3 ½ pounds (1.6 kilograms) sirloin tip roast
2 10 ½-ounce (300-gram) cans beef consommé (undiluted)

DIRECTIONS: Cook meat uncovered in preheated 450–500°F (230–260°C) degree oven for 30 minutes (do not use glass baking dish). Turn off oven and quickly pour consommé over roast. Close door and let roast sit in oven for 2 full hours. DO NOT OPEN OVEN DOOR! Carve in thin slices and serve with crusty French rolls. Give each person small individual bowls of juice to dip their sandwiches in.

My friend Sharon shared this recipe with me.

aunt susie's tips:
*For larger roasts, add another can
of consommé and allow 3 hours
in the oven.*

I have showed you all things, how that so labouring ye ought to support the weak, and to remember the words of the Lord Jesus, how he said, It is more blessed to give than to receive.

ACTS 20:35

In this strange and wonderful world of ours, we hear a lot about single moms and their struggles to earn a good living and raise their children, many without the support of their children's fathers. Well, I am proud to say that two of my nephews have joint custody of their children and have taken on the responsibility of sharing the care and support of their children. It is so good to see these young men with their children and the close ties that they are developing with them. These men are setting a good example for their children and others who know them. All of us parents know how difficult it can be raising children and what a thankless job it often is, and being a single parent takes even more tenacity and endurance. When the children are older, they will come to appreciate the sacrifices their fathers made for them and the love they have for them. May all parents enter this responsibility of child caring ready to provide both financial and emotional support.

The support from God for us is never-ending. Let us support the children in our lives as He supports us, His children.

SLOPPY JOES

Single parents can whip up this kid-pleasing favorite even after a long day's work.

SERVES 4 TO 6

—◦◦◦—

1 pound (455 grams) ground chuck
1 teaspoon minced garlic
$\frac{1}{3}$ cup (50 grams) chopped onion
$\frac{1}{2}$ teaspoon oregano
$\frac{1}{2}$ teaspoon dry mustard

1 bay leaf
Pinch pepper
1 10-ounce (280-gram) can tomato soup
2 tablespoons ketchup

DIRECTIONS: Sauté meat with garlic and onion. Add remaining ingredients and simmer until fairly thick. Serve open-faced over hamburger buns and top with cheese, if desired.

Be strong and of a good courage, fear not, nor be afraid of them: for the LORD thy God, he it is that doth go with thee; he will not fail thee, nor forsake thee.

DEUTERONOMY 31:6

When I was attending college in Cincinnati, Ohio, my friend and I had part-time jobs working at a department store downtown. About four times a week we took turns driving to work. We always parked in a nearby parking garage for our convenience. This particular day, we had parked on the sixth floor. We stepped into the elevator, which was already occupied by an older man. We hit the button, and the elevator took us to the first floor. When the elevator stopped, however, the elevator door wouldn't open. We pressed the Open Door button frantically, but it would not budge. There was no phone in the elevator, so we rang the alarm button for help. As we waited for help to arrive, this man who was in the elevator with us pulled out a bottle of gin, took a swig, and started telling us dirty jokes. We were very young, naive, and very embarrassed. I'm not sure if we were more frightened of him or of being stuck in the elevator! We tried to change the subject, but to no avail. He went on and on. My friend and I huddled together. We were so glad that we had each other. After what seemed like forever, we heard noises from outside the door. Someone had finally come to our rescue.

Sometimes when our fear is so overwhelming, it is hard to remember that we are in God's care. Call on our Lord for the courage you need in times of fear.

HUNGARIAN GOULASH

If you're afraid to cook for company, start with this recipe—
it's mistake-proof and perfect for entertaining.

SERVES 6 TO 8

1¹/₂–2 pounds (680–910 grams) stew beef

³/₄ cup (180 grams) ketchup

1 tablespoon brown sugar

2 tablespoons Worcestershire sauce

2 teaspoons paprika

¹/₂ teaspoon dry mustard

1¹/₂ cups (360 milliliters) water

2 tablespoons flour mixed well with 2 tablespoons water

Sour cream

DIRECTIONS: Place meat in a large pot with all ingredients except flour mixture and sour cream. Bring to boil, and simmer for about 2 hours. Add flour mixture and stir to thicken sauce. Serve over egg noodles. Place dollop of sour cream on top.

My sister Marilyn shared this recipe with me.

O give thanks unto the LORD; for he is good;
for his mercy endureth for ever.

1 CHRONICLES 16:34

As a mother of three children and a grandmother of one, I have always worried about their safety. You moms know about that protective instinct we have. Many years ago, my then two-year-old daughter, Joelle, had a freakish accident during the early hours of the morning. I was awakened by the distant but urgent cry of "Mommy!" I followed Joelle's cries for help and found her outside the house. I later learned that she went into her brother's second-story bedroom and hopped onto his bed. Since his bedroom window screen had fallen out during the early morning storm, she put her hand out the open window to feel the rain. Then, horror of horrors, she fell close to twelve feet directly below the upstairs window—in between the cement gutter and the rock garden! Trying to contain my panic, I rushed her to the hospital. She had broken her leg, but other than being quite shaken up, she was just fine! She wore a cast for eight weeks and her leg healed beautifully. I thanked God over and over. Although very memorable for me, this incident is only like a grain of sand when we think of all the many, many times blessings occur in our lives.

Take only five minutes a day to ponder your blessings, and you will be astounded all that you take for granted. As you say a little prayer of thanks, include those who are less fortunate.

BEEF FONDUE

All my family members are grateful when I fix beef fondue for dinner. I usually reserve making it for special occasions.

SERVES 8 TO 10

4 pounds (1.8 kilograms) beef sirloin steak, cut into 1-inch cubes

1 1/2 cups (360 milliliters) cranberry/raspberry juice

1/2 cup (120 milliliters) grape juice or red wine

MUSTARD MAYONNAISE SAUCE:

1 cup (235 grams) mayonnaise

2 hard-boiled eggs, chopped

2 tablespoons dried parsley flakes

1 tablespoon mustard

1/4 cup (25 grams) chopped green onions, optional

DIRECTIONS: In a large bowl, combine juices and meat. Cover and refrigerate. Marinate meat for 2–3 hours. Ten minutes before dinner, fill an electric fondue pot with corn oil (a little over halfway). Set the temperature to 375°F (190°C). Drain beef. Enjoy yourself while you all cook your own dinner. Serve with Mustard Mayonnaise Sauce.

aunt susie's tips:

A salad and baked potato make a good accompaniment. Also, if you want to make it more tender, use filet mignon instead of sirloin. Vegetable oil can be substituted for corn oil. I usually serve beef and chicken fondue together with this sauce and the Apricot Sauce found with the chicken fondue recipe.

*In that day will I raise up the tabernacle
of David that is fallen, and close up the
breaches thereof; and I will raise up his ruins,
and I will build it as in the days of old.*

AMOS 9:11

The first house my husband and I bought was a fairly new two-story home in Virginia Beach. We owned the home for only eight months, but during that time, it seemed that everything that could go wrong did. When we first moved in, the dishwasher caught fire the first time I used it. I then bought a portable dishwasher until the repairman could come, and the water came pouring out of it during the rinse cycle, flooding the kitchen. Then the clothes dryer burned up, ruining all the clothes inside. The television went kaput; the refrigerator took its last breath; and the washing machine kept filling up with water and ended up overflowing into the family room. Next our well went dry, and the water that we did have was coming from a leak in our dining room ceiling. We had to repair our fence three different times—first a storm blew it down, next a neighborhood boy ran a big cable spool through it, and finally it caught fire. At the same time, I had to take my husband to the emergency room two different times: once for an allergic reaction to shellfish and another time for a gallbladder attack. It may have been a blessing when my husband got his orders from the Navy that he was being reassigned. We were more than happy to move and begin again.

We usually know when we need to repair our homes, but we are more reluctant to repair our lives. Ask God to assist you when you go about repairing your life. Like a well-maintained home, we need to do a maintenance check on ourselves as well.

BEEF STROGANOFF

You won't need to patch up this recipe. It's great just the way it is.

SERVES 8

———ᔈᔈᔈ———

- 1 16-ounce (455-gram) package egg noodles
- 2 pounds (900 grams) beef strips, as for stir-frying
- 1/2 cup (80 grams) chopped onion
- 1 teaspoon minced garlic
- 1 1/2 cups (360 milliliters) beef broth
- 2 tablespoons ketchup
- 2 cups (140 grams) sliced mushrooms
- 2 tablespoons cranberry or grape juice
- 3 tablespoons flour
- 3 tablespoons milk or half-and-half
- 1 cup (230 grams) sour cream

DIRECTIONS: Cook noodles as directed; drain and keep warm. Spray skillet with nonstick cooking spray and sauté meat, onion, and garlic over high heat until brown. Turn down to medium-high heat and add beef broth, ketchup, and mushrooms and juice. Reduce heat to low. Cover and simmer for about 5 minutes or until tender. Mix flour with milk or half-and-half, blending until smooth. Slowly stir flour mixture into beef. Heat to boiling, stirring constantly until thickened to desired consistency. Lower heat and stir in sour cream. Serve over hot noodles.

My friend and neighbor April shared this recipe with me.

In like manner also, that women adorn themselves
in modest apparel…

1 TIMOTHY 2:9

Modesty. Remember that word? It was the first day of summer, and my cousin and I wanted to go swimming at the local park. Mom didn't really want me to go, but after we kept on bugging her, she finally relented and took us to the pool, where we met some friends. We were having such a good time when . . . boom. I went down the slide, and a friend came down too soon after, hitting me on the side and knocking me under the water. Two friends pulled me out of the water, as I couldn't move. The lifeguard came over and thought I was okay since I had no external bleeding or bruises. My cousin called my poor mom, and she came right away. My friends helped me into the backseat of the car, and mom headed out, but she was first heading for home to get a robe before taking me to the hospital. She wanted to make sure I was "decent," as she said. Mom wanted to make sure I was modestly dressed before I went to the hospital. I fully recovered and now we laugh when we think of Mom and her concern for my modesty.

Modesty in all things is one of God's virtues. In this ever-changing world, don't forget to teach this tried-and-true value.

MEXICAN LOAF

For a modest meal, prepare this Mexican loaf. Kids love it.

SERVES 6 TO 8

1 loaf Vienna or Italian bread, sliced in half lengthwise

1 container taco meat sauce, already cooked and seasoned

2 tomatoes, sliced

1 8-ounce (235-milliliter) can sliced black olives, drained

2 cups (230 grams) shredded cheese, Mexican blend

Jalapeno peppers, optional

2–4 tablespoons margarine, softened

DIRECTIONS: Put both pieces of bread on cookie sheet lined with aluminum foil. Spread bread with thin layer of margarine. Spread meat mixture on top of buttered bread. Top with tomato slices and black olives. Sprinkle with cheese. Bake at 375°F (190°C) for 7–10 minutes. Serve with salsa and sour cream.

My friend Vicki shared this recipe with me.

Honour thy father and thy mother:
that thy days may be long upon the land
which the LORD thy God giveth thee.

Exodus 20:12

*E*very once in a while I run into someone who says, "I'm having such a good time with my children and enjoying them so much." And they're talking about their teenagers. When I hear that, I can't believe it. I had a very trying time when my children were teenagers. They became very disrespectful and disobedient and went through a very rebellious period. Even though I enjoyed some of my children's teen years, I have to say I was miserable a lot of the time. When my oldest daughter was sixteen and had her own car, she took the car one night without permission and didn't come back for hours. I worried and stewed all night until she came home. I took her car keys for a month to teach her a lesson. I never stopped loving my children, but sometimes I just didn't like them. Fortunately, they eventually did grow out of their terrible teens and now appreciate and respect me once more. All's well that ends well.

Honoring our parents is expected by God, and that goes for us adults with our older parents as well. Remember to treat your parents, no matter what their age, with the honor they deserve.

TACO PIE

Drop by and surprise your mom and dad with this taco pie
for dinner some evening soon.

SERVES 6

—◦◦◦—

CRUST:
1 can Pillsbury corn bread,
  rolled out

FILLING:
1 pound (455 grams) lean ground
  beef
1 cup (260 grams) chunky salsa
1 cup (115 grams) shredded
  Co-Jack cheese

TOPPING:
1 cup (55 grams) shredded lettuce
½ cup (90 grams) chopped tomato
¼ cup (45 grams) sliced black olives
Sour cream

DIRECTIONS: Lightly spray pie pan with nonstick cooking spray. Roll
out dough on a floured surface, and lay crust in pan. Brown meat and
drain well. Combine salsa with meat. Pour into pie. Sprinkle with cheese.
Bake for 15 minutes at 375°F (190°C) or until cheese is melted. Top
with lettuce, tomato, olives, and sour cream.

My friend and neighbor April shared this recipe with me.

CHICKEN DINNERS

Greater love hath no man than this,
that a man lay down his life for his friends.

JOHN 15:13

*B*ack in the early 1970s when we were living in Norfolk, Virginia, we became friends with some wonderful people, one family being Sharon and Dick and their three children. Since both of our husbands were in the Navy and out to sea quite often, Sharon and I spent a lot of time together. Both of us shared a love of good food and cooking. We were always trying new recipes and coming up with new ideas for old recipes. Once in a while we would take turns creating these wonderful dinners for each other. It was like going out to eat in a gourmet restaurant. We set the table with nice silverware and dishes and fed the kids early, so they could play while we ate and had our nice dinner. What great fun we had. When we moved to Ohio, all of us cried as we were going to miss our dear friends, and so we have. Now that I am writing this cookbook, I called and asked my dear friend for some recipes. I have included quite a few for you to enjoy.

Friends are sent to us by God in so many ways at so many times. What would life be like without them? Call an old friend today.

HONEY MUSTARD CHICKEN

Call a friend over to share this dinner.
You'll have plenty of time to visit as it cooks.

SERVES 6

—⟨∾∾⟩—

1 stick butter or margarine
½ cup (125 grams) prepared mustard
1 cup (340 grams) honey

1 teaspoon curry powder
  (or more, according to taste)
6 chicken breasts

DIRECTIONS: Melt butter in a saucepan. Add mustard, honey, and curry powder. Stir well. Place chicken breasts in a greased baking dish. Spread mixture over chicken, adding remaining sauce to pan. Bake at 350°F (180°C) for 1 hour. Great served with yellow rice.

My friend Sharon shared this recipe with me.

He that hath a bountiful eye shall be blessed;
for he giveth of his bread to the poor.

PROVERBS 22:9

*P*eg had to quit school in the sixth grade to help her aunt and uncle. She had to leave home and move in with her relatives and cook for the thrashers on the farm. Later, she met my dad, married, and had four girls. She was a great cook and always cooked for an army, as my dad said. One day, Mother and my older sister Lois, who was about five years old at the time, answered the door to find a vagabond who was begging for food. Lois tugged at Mother's skirt, saying, "Mama, we better feed him. It may be Jesus in disguise." Mother invited him in for dinner, and this was the beginning of many souls in need stopping by our house to be fed by my mother. They loved her cooking, especially her pies, which she prided herself on.

Those of us who have more are expected by God to spread our good fortune around. Plan to help someone in need very soon. Remember "it could be Jesus in disguise."

CHICKEN POT PIE

Someone in need could use this pot pie. Make several
to freeze for a needy family in your neighborhood.

SERVES 6 TO 8

⅓ cup (85 grams) margarine

⅓ cup (40 grams) flour

2 tablespoons minced onion

¼ teaspoon pepper

1 ¾ cups (420 milliliters) chicken
broth (canned or soup base
added to water)

⅔ cup (160 milliliters) milk

2 cups (280 grams) cooked chicken
cut into bite-sized cubes

1 16-ounce (455-gram) package
frozen vegetables

1 package refrigerated piecrusts
(let sit at room temperature for
5 minutes before using)

Pinch of celery seed

DIRECTIONS: Melt margarine in saucepan over medium heat. Blend
in flour, onion, and pepper and cook until bubbly. Add chicken broth and
milk. Heat until boiling and boil for one minute. Remove from heat and
add chicken and frozen vegetables; stir together. Place one piecrust in an
11-inch greased pie pan. Pour in filling. Place second piecrust on top, and
pinch edges together. Sprinkle with a little bit of celery seed, and cut slits
in top to let steam escape. Bake at 425°F (220°C) for 30–35 minutes.

aunt susie's tips:
*This is great with a salad. You can buy cooked chicken breast
at your local supermarket to cut down on cooking time.*

*For I will have respect unto you, and make
you fruitful, and multiply you, and establish
my covenant with you.*

LEVITICUS 26:9

*I*n my humble opinion, I keep saying that the loss of respect is one
of the causes of many of today's problems. Not only respect for
each other, but also respect for ourselves. As a young child, I remember
addressing all adults with a title such as "Mr.," "Mrs.," "Miss," "Aunt,"
"Uncle," and so forth. One evening my future brother-in-law Paul was
coming to dinner and bringing his father with him. Before dinner his
father, Mr. Munier, told me I could call him "Energetic Eddie." He
was a really pleasant man, always bubbly, and he looked like a little
teddy bear. When all of us were seated at the dinner table and prayers
were said, we started passing the food around the table. I looked at
Mr. Munier and said, "Energetic Eddie, would you please pass the
potatoes?" My father and my mother both looked up at me in disbelief,
and my father asked for an apology and sent me to my room. Even
though Energetic Eddie insisted that it was his fault and that he had
asked me to call him that, my father said, "She knows better." The
next time it was definitely "Mr. Munier."

*Respecting our elders is counted upon by God, but it shouldn't stop there.
We should all treat each other with mutual respect.*

PECAN CHICKEN

This sophisticated Southern-style pecan chicken is
worthy of your guests and your respect.

SERVES 4

8 boneless, skinless chicken tenders

1 egg, beaten

2 cups (240 grams) pecan pieces

Vegetable oil for cooking

$\frac{1}{3}$ cup (90 milliliters) chutney

$\frac{1}{4}$ cup (85 grams) honey

DIRECTIONS: Dip tenders into egg and coat both sides with pecans. Over medium heat, brown chicken on both sides in vegetable oil. Reduce heat and cook chicken until done. Combine chutney and honey in small bowl, mixing well. Remove chicken from pan and put on microwaveable dish. Spread chutney mixture on chicken and microwave for 15 seconds on high.

aunt susie's tips:
*Serve with a salad and
fresh vegetable.*

And ye yourselves like unto men that wait for their lord, when he will return from the wedding; that when he cometh and knocketh, they may open unto him immediately.

LUKE 12:36

Have you ever had a premonition or a feeling that something bad is going to happen? In high school, I was sitting in my English class when someone knocked at the door. Somehow I knew that knock was meant for me, and indeed it was. My mother, who had been admitted to the hospital a few days earlier, had gone into convulsions and was expected to die. I rode to the hospital in a state of shock. It was too much when the doctor said we should pray for her to pass quickly. This was my mom. I didn't want to lose her. I had just visited her the night before at the hospital, and I had told the nurse that she was not acting right and something was wrong. They told me it was the effects of the medicine they had given her. Mom died late that morning. The good thing is that my mother's suffering stopped, and I know she is looking down on me from her serene place in heaven.

Death can knock at our door any time. Live your life in the presence of God so that you are ready when the time comes.

PEANUTTY CHICKEN

Make this dinner for someone who is grieving for a loved one.

SERVES 4 TO 5

½ cup (130 grams) peanut butter

3 tablespoons brown sugar

½ cup (120 milliliters) coconut milk

1 teaspoon chili powder

½ teaspoon hot sauce

1 tablespoon oil

10 boneless, skinless chicken tenders

½ teaspoon minced garlic

½ teaspoon fresh ginger, chopped

DIRECTIONS: In small bowl, combine peanut butter, brown sugar, coconut milk, chili powder, and hot sauce. Set aside. Add oil to skillet and sauté chicken, garlic, and ginger. Stir fry until crisp and golden. Add peanut butter mixture and toss with chicken. Simmer for 2 to 3 minutes. Serve over a bed of rice.

For I was my father's son, tender and only beloved
in the sight of my mother.

PROVERBS 4:3

They say a mother's love can conquer anything, and I believe it's true—but sometimes it may take a few minutes for that instinct to kick in. I was at a park with my daughter when she was around six or seven years old. There were a lot of children there, and they were all gathered down by the creek. One of the children had seen a snake, and all of them were fascinated, hunting for the snake and waiting for it to make its appearance once more. My daughter was sitting on the grass on the side of the creek when all of a sudden the snake crawled right across her legs. I was right behind her, looking down, and I saw the snake at once. I instinctively jumped away. That's right—away! I hate snakes! Once my daughter saw the snake, she started screaming, and at that moment nothing mattered. I forced myself to be brave, and I pulled her up in my arms and away from the snake. A mother's love can conquer all, but as I said, sometimes it takes a moment for the instinct to kick in.

Mothers share a unique bond with their children. Remember to give thanks to God for your loving mother.

CRACKER CHICKEN

This is an old-fashioned recipe that screams "Mom's good home cooking." Share it with someone in need of a little comfort food.

SERVES 4

8 boneless, skinless chicken tenders

2 eggs, beaten

2 rolls of buttery snack crackers, crushed

DIRECTIONS: Dip chicken tenders in egg, and coat with cracker crumbs. Spray large baking dish well with nonstick cooking spray. Bake at 450°F (230°C) for 10 minutes; turn over and cook for an additional 10 minutes.

aunt susie's tips:
You can fry the chicken in a skillet if you prefer.

And the LORD spoke unto you out of the midst of the fire: ye heard the voice of the words, but saw no similitude; only ye heard a voice.

DEUTERONOMY 4:12

When my sister Anita's husband Jim died in 1993, it came as a shock to all of us. We had just visited them recently, and he seemed in really good health. As soon as we heard the news, we left to be with my sister and her family for a couple of days. On the way over, my husband and I were talking and reminiscing about the times that we had shared with him over the years. I was driving, and Larry started falling asleep while reading his book. I had the radio on and was listening to some soothing music. While I was driving along on the interstate, a strange feeling came over me. I heard a voice talking to me that sounded like Jim's. It gave me quite a scare at first. I looked over at Larry, and he was still asleep. Then I heard his voice again. It told me to tell Anita that he was just fine, and then it repeated the same thing, and that was it. Later, I told my sister about it in hopes that it would help comfort her, and I think it did.

How many times have we heard God's voice and didn't listen? Be a better listener—both to God and to others.

RUSSIAN CHICKEN

Whenever I make this recipe, one of Jim's favorites,
I know God is reminding me to listen.

SERVES 6 TO 8

6–8 chicken breasts, boneless
and skinless

1 cup (245 grams) Russian dressing

1 cup (320 grams) apricot preserves

1 envelope dry onion soup mix

¹⁄₂ cup (120 milliliters) water

1 8-ounce (235-milliliter) can sliced
water chestnuts

1 20-ounce (460-gram) can
pineapple chunks, drained

2 onions, quartered

DIRECTIONS: Place chicken in a greased 9" × 13" baking dish.
Combine remaining ingredients in a bowl. Pour mixture over chicken.
Bake at 350°F (180°C) for 60 to 75 minutes until brown on top.

My sister Anita shared this recipe with me.

And he saith unto them, Why are ye fearful,
O ye of little faith? Then he arose, and rebuked the
winds and the sea; and there was a great calm.

MATTHEW 8:26

Recently, my sister Anita's faith was tested while riding in the car with my husband, Larry, and I in New York. We were just leaving Ellis Island, where Anita and I had seen the spot where our father had first set foot in the United States after immigrating back in 1911. We were driving back to Salem, Massachusetts, that evening so Anita and her husband could catch a plane early in the morning. We had left later than expected, and the rain was really coming down, reducing visibility on the road. I usually drive in the metropolitan areas, but this time Larry was doing the driving. Normally, Larry follows the speed limit to a fault, but he was on a mission—to get us back to the hotel by midnight. I didn't realize how terrified my sister was until I turned around and saw her clutching her rosary for dear life, praying softly to herself. Well, Anita's faith paid off for all of us, and we all were very happy to arrive safely at the hotel. As we walked in, Anita said, "I love you and your husband dearly, but I'll never set foot in a car with him at the wheel again!"

When you get scared, hold fast to your faith in God, and He will see you through.

ORANGE CHICKEN

This orange chicken will see you through the
dinner hour on the toughest of days.

SERVES 4

4 boneless, skinless chicken breasts
1/4 teaspoon garlic powder
Salt and pepper to taste
1 tablespoon Dijon mustard

1/4 cup (60 milliliters) orange juice
1 teaspoon dried orange peel
Minced fresh parsley

DIRECTIONS: Spray a large skillet with nonstick cooking spray.
Sprinkle chicken with garlic powder, salt, and pepper; brown in hot skillet
2 to 3 minutes, turning once. Combine mustard, orange juice, and dried
orange peel. Pour over chicken; cover and simmer for 7 minutes. Remove
chicken to plate. Cook pan juices until reduced by half. Pour over chicken.
Garnish with fresh minced parsley.

My friend Sharon shared this recipe with me.

And they knew not that Joseph understood them;
for he spoke unto them by an interpreter.

GENESIS 42:23

Communicating with people who speak another language can be very difficult. When my husband and I were on our Mediterranean odyssey with our friends, David and Margo, we had some interesting experiences with communication. While we were in Egypt, a guide found us walking by ourselves and immediately attached himself to us. He spoke limited English and interpreted for us. I wanted to find some Egyptian sheets. He took us through the alleys and narrow passageways of many bazaars. We found beautiful sheets that were embroidered, but they were too small. I needed king-size sheets, which was hard to communicate, and all they had were plain white sheets in large sizes. The guide said these could be embroidered right away. We bought the sheets, and off we went with our guide. We soon found rows of men and women seated at their sewing machines, stitching at phenomenal speeds. They spoke no English, and we spoke no Egyptian, so we communicated through the guide. We smiled at each other throughout and watched intently as these women went about their task, proud of their craft. We tipped them well. Their faces beamed as they handed us the magnificent pieces of linen, which we will treasure forever.

God encourages us to communicate with people as best we can, no matter what the challenges. Make an effort to reach out to others with compassion and understanding.

Curry Chicken

The universal language of food is easily appreciated
with this savory chicken dish.

Serves 6

2 tablespoons butter or margarine

$^1/_2$ cup (80 grams) chopped onion

2 tablespoons flour

1 teaspoon curry powder

1 cup (240 milliliters) chicken broth

2 cups (280 grams) cooked chicken
breasts, cut into bite-sized pieces

$^1/_2$ cup (115 grams) sour cream

1 10-ounce (280-gram) can cream
of chicken soup

DIRECTIONS: Heat butter in skillet. Add onion and sauté, but do not brown. Mix in flour and curry powder. Add chicken broth and stir until the mixture thickens. Cook for 5 minutes. Add chicken, sour cream, and cream of chicken soup and continue cooking for an additional 5 minutes. Serve over rice.

aunt susie's tips:
*I love Earl Grey's chutney and
always serve it with this recipe.*

Finally, be ye all of one mind, having
compassion one of another, love as brethren,
be pitiful, be courteous.

1 PETER 3:8

When I was young, I was very accident prone, and my mother was always sympathetic. I was always hurting myself somehow or another, and my mother was endlessly patient with me. She told me to be careful, but she encouraged me to participate in activities. On one particular spring day, I was skating down the sidewalk with a couple of friends, having a great time, when all of a sudden, I went up in the air and then down with a crash. I was so busy chattering away with my friends that I hadn't seen a large crack in the sidewalk. I was sprawled out on the ground and in severe pain; my friends helped me to my feet. My right arm was throbbing, and I started crying. My mom rushed me to our family doctor, and off to the hospital I went to get my broken arm and broken wrist set in a cast. My mother took care of me that day, and every other, with lots of love and sympathy.

God's compassion is omnipresent. Learn to be tenderhearted in your dealings with others.

Ginger Chicken Stir-Fry

Lend a charitable hand to a friend in distress
with this effortless dinner.

Serves 4

8 tablespoons soy sauce

2 tablespoons sherry

$^1/_4$ teaspoon ginger

$^1/_4$ cup (55 grams) brown sugar

3 boneless, skinless chicken breasts,
cut into bite-sized pieces

4 ounces (115 grams) fresh sliced
mushrooms

1 8-ounce (235-milliliter) can sliced
water chestnuts, drained

$^1/_2$ teaspoon minced garlic

1 5-ounce (140-gram) package fresh
pea pods

1 tablespoon corn starch mixed
with 2 tablespoons cold water

DIRECTIONS: Mix soy sauce, sherry, ginger, and brown sugar together
in a small bowl. Heat oil and stir-fry chicken breasts. Add mushrooms,
water chestnuts, garlic, and pea pods. Add soy sauce and sherry mixture
toward end of stir-fry. Thicken with cornstarch and water.

I will praise thee for ever, because thou hast done it: and I will wait on thy name; for it is good before thy saints.

PSALM 52:9

In the early years of my marriage, my husband was out to sea quite often in his Navy job, and I had to learn to do many things for myself. I became my own "jill-of-all-trades" to save money and fix things that broke. I bought myself a do-it-yourself book, and I was on my way—unclogging drains, changing fixtures, hanging shelves, you name it! I tried to do my big projects while he was gone on long business trips, and I would usually have them completed before he came home. One time, however, I bit off more than I could chew. After visiting my sister and brother-in-law at their home and seeing the beautiful genuine wood floor they had installed, I decided I had to have it—and would do it myself. As Larry planned for a month-long trip, I planned for "the big one." It was a daunting task, but I was sure I could have it all done on time. As soon as Larry left, the groundbreaking began. I ripped out the carpets and knocked down a wall that was in my way. Little did I know what I was in for! Once I was in too deep, I realized there was no way I would have this project done in time to surprise my husband. Oh, he was surprised, all right, when he stepped into the house and saw the ripped-out floors and the wall-less family room, but not in the way I wanted him to be.

Thanks be to God for giving us the determination and the will to complete those tasks we start. If you're struggling to complete a project, ask God to spur you on.

Chicken Bundles

Take these scrumptious eat-as-you-go bundles to someone working hard to meet a deadline. They'll love you for it.

SERVES 8

2 teaspoons butter or margarine, melted

1 3-ounce (85-gram) package cream cheese, softened

2 cups (280 grams) chicken breast, cooked and cut into bite-sized pieces

$\frac{1}{8}$ teaspoon pepper

2 tablespoons minced onion

3 tablespoons milk

1 small jar of mushroom pieces, drained, optional

1 box refrigerated pie crusts (2 per box), cut into quarters

DIRECTIONS: In a medium bowl, blend melted butter and cream cheese together. Then add chicken, pepper, onion, and milk. If desired, add mushrooms. Divide chicken mixture equally and place in the center of each pie wedge. Pull edges together and pinch. You may need to moisten the edges with water to make them stick. Cut slits in the top to let steam escape. Place on greased baking sheet and bake at 375°F (190°C) for 20–25 minutes.

My friends Jennifer and Kathi shared this recipe with me.

Be completely humble and gentle; be patient, bearing with one another in love.

EPHESIANS 4:2

When my husband was a junior officer in the Navy, we were invited to a dinner party at a senior officer's home. Several other couples were in attendance, and the senior officer's wife took great pride in their newly furnished house. After the main dinner course, the party moved from the dining table to the living room for coffee and dessert. The hostess walked around and passed out dessert plates containing portions of lemon meringue pie. I lifted my fork from the plate to my mouth. The pressure of my fork on the pie crust caused my dessert portion to split and fly in three directions—one piece on the rug, one piece on my dress, and another on the sport coat of a guest sitting next to me. In horror, I rose to apologize and, in the process, dropped my meringue-covered fork on another person's shoe. Someone broke the stunned silence by making a light-hearted remark: "Well, this might be a good time for your baby-sitter to call." Within two minutes, the phone rang. It was the baby-sitter, asking us to come home because of a minor accident involving one of our children. We exited quietly.

Just when we are a little too proud, God steps in and humbles us. Practice the virtue of humility.

CHEESY CHICKEN ENCHILADAS

This humble dinner is a snap. Cook some up tonight.

MAKES 8

4 cooked chicken breasts

1 onion, minced

2 1/2 cups (290 grams) shredded Co-Jack cheese

2 8-ounce (235 milliliter) cans enchilada sauce

8 flour tortillas

DIRECTIONS: Shred the cooked chicken. Mix onion, 3/4 cup cheese, and 1/2 can enchilada sauce; add shredded chicken. Fill tortillas and roll, placing them in a 9" × 13" baking dish. Cover with remaining sauce and cheese. Bake at 350°F (180°C) for 15 to 20 minutes.

My friend and neighbor April shared this recipe with me.

aunt susie's tips:
Top with olives, tomatoes, and sour cream for a nice treat.

*...for then thou shalt make thy way prosperous,
and then thou shalt have good success.*

JOSHUA 1:8

*T*here are all kinds of ways to measure success. For me, one of the most successful women I know is my dear friend Sharnell. When Sharnell came to work with me part time at my store, she also had two other jobs, but she still helped me out when she was dead tired. She was a good, loving mother whose main concern was to raise her daughters. She made a warm and loving home for them, and she was there for them when they needed her. It wasn't an easy road. Now she is still working too hard, caring for two grandchildren during the week and holding down a part-time job as well. Her husband of eight years is a terrific support to her, and they complement each other well. I count them both as my dear, wonderful friends. The love and respect of her family and many friends attests to her success throughout her life.

The successes in your life come from God, who makes all things possible. Thank Him.

JAMBALAYA

This chicken jambalaya makes a success of any
party—it's good, inexpensive, and fun.

SERVES 6 TO 8

2 cups (280 grams) boneless, skinless chicken breast, cut into bite-sized pieces

1 cup (160 grams) chopped onion

1 cup (150 grams) chopped green pepper

2 teaspoons minced garlic

2 tablespoons salad oil

1 cup (110 grams) cooked ham, cubed

2 16-ounce (475-milliliter) cans tomatoes

1 cup (185 grams) long grain rice, uncooked

1 1/2 cups (360 milliliters) chicken broth

1/2 teaspoon thyme

1 tablespoon chopped parsley

DIRECTIONS: Sauté chicken, onion, green pepper, and garlic in oil in skillet until tender. Stir in ham and cook for 5 minutes. Add all remaining ingredients. Put in a greased 9" × 13" casserole dish. Cover with aluminum foil and bake at 350°F (180°C) for 1 hour.

My friend Shar shared this recipe with me.

...and I have prevailed...

GENESIS 30:8

As we were moving my son's bed into his new room, we noticed that the heating vent cover was missing. With his prized Mickey Mouse radio in hand, he went to have a closer look. He tripped over a box on the floor and dropped the radio, which fell right into the vent, tumbling from the second story all the way down to the basement. Bang, clang, we heard as it went. He was beside himself with grief. How were we going to get it? We were right in the middle of moving things, and I wanted to put it off, but my son was determined to reclaim his radio. He found a flashlight and saw the radio at the very bottom of the vent, way, way down. He scavenged around for tools. He returned with some wire hangers and duct tape. We untwisted and straightened the hangers and taped them together with the duct tape, creating a long pole with a loop at the end. Then we set out to go fishing for the radio. Luckily, the radio had a handle that we could loop onto. Over an hour later, we pulled up the radio. Our son's perseverance had prevailed: he had his precious radio back.

With God's help, you may prevail with the challenges in this life. Count on Him.

Peachy Chicken

After a long day of overcoming obstacles,
all is peachy again when you serve this fruity chicken.

MAKES 8

—⟨∞⟩—

1 10-ounce (280-gram) box couscous

1 1/4 cups (300 milliliters) chicken broth

8 chicken tenders, boneless and skinless

1 teaspoon mustard

1/2 cup (120 grams) peach preserves

2 tablespoons orange juice

2 tablespoons honey

1/4 cup (40 grams) raisins

1/4 cup (40 grams) dried apricots, diced

2 teaspoons sweetened orange juice

DIRECTIONS: Start couscous, following directions on package, substituting chicken broth for water. Spray skillet with nonstick cooking spray and brown chicken, turning once. In a separate bowl, mix mustard, peach preserves, 2 tablespoons orange juice, and honey. Add mixture to chicken, cooking for an additional 5 minutes. When couscous is finished, add raisins, dried apricots, and sweetened orange juice. Serve chicken with couscous.

Seek the LORD and his strength,
seek his face continually.

1 CHRONICLES 16:11

Kathi was going to school to become a physician's assistant. Her fifteen-year marriage had ended, and she had two children who were about twelve and fifteen years old. But Kathi went on to receive her degree and started working for the U.S. government, helping people with addictions—drugs, alcohol, and so forth. She has been doing this now for nearly thirteen years, going day after day, dealing with this high-stress job, caring for people. Her fortitude is amazing. She keeps on going with a great attitude, always wanting to help people improve their lives. When I think of Luke the physician, I think of Kathi and the role she has in the lives of the many people she is trying to help. Kathi has amazing strength to keep on going, and she keeps on going no matter what.

What great strength we receive from the Lord when we seek it. We must call upon Him to help us overcome our addictions.

CREAMY ENCHILADAS

Prepare this spicy dish for someone struggling to overcome
an addiction, as a gesture of support and understanding.

SERVES 4 TO 6

1 medium bag of tortilla chips

1 8-ounce (235-milliliter) carton of
sour cream

1/3 cup (80 milliliters) milk

1 10-ounce (280-gram) can cream
of chicken soup

1 4-ounce (120-milliliter) can
chopped green chilies

1 small onion, chopped

2 cups (280 grams) cooked chicken,
cut into bite-sized pieces

1 8-ounce (230-gram) package
shredded Monterey Jack cheese

Jalapeños and taco sauce may
also be added

DIRECTIONS: Place 1/2 package tortilla chips in the bottom of a greased
casserole dish. In a medium bowl, mix sour cream, milk, soup, green
chilies, and onion. Pour half of mixture over tortilla chips. Add half of the
chicken and sprinkle with half of the cheese. Repeat the layers and finish
with the cheese. Bake covered at 350°F (180°C) for 30–45 minutes.

My friend Kathi shared this recipe with me.

aunt susie's tips:
*This recipe would taste good with
other kinds of white cheese as well.*

Therefore, brethren, stand fast, and hold the traditions which ye have been taught, whether by word, or our epistle.

2 THESSALONIANS 2:15

*F*amily rituals and traditions create a sense of togetherness and being part of a special unit or group. These special times have been passed on to us from our family, and we continue to pass them on to our children, and hopefully they will do the same and keep passing them down over time. Traditions can be as simple as going out to a movie and dinner once in a while with your children or taking them out for a special treat. One of our favorites is chicken fondue every Christmas Eve. Also at Christmastime, my husband takes the adult children and young ones to see the Nutcracker. Think about the traditions in your family. I know I've been thinking about it, and I'm going to start some simple new ones by getting together for dinner with the whole family at least once a month.

God is a major part of many of our traditional celebrations. Make Him a part of your daily life as well.

CHICKEN FONDUE

I always fix this meal as a tradition for our
Christmas Eve dinner. Make it yours.

SERVES 4 TO 6

2 pounds (900 grams) chicken
breast, cut into 1-inch cubes

¼ cup (60 milliliters) soy sauce

⅓ cup (80 milliliters) sherry

1 teaspoon ginger

APRICOT SAUCE:

2 cups (460 grams) sour cream

1 16-ounce (475-milliliter) jar
apricot preserves

⅛ teaspoon ground ginger

⅛ teaspoon curry powder

DIRECTIONS: In a large bowl, combine first four ingredients. Cover
and refrigerate. Marinate chicken for 2–3 hours. Ten minutes before
dinner, fill an electric fondue pot with corn oil (a little over halfway).
Set the temperature to 375°F (190°C). Drain marinade before cooking.
Enjoy yourself while you all cook your own dinner. Mix all ingredients
for the Apricot Sauce together well. Refrigerate until time to serve.

aunt susie's tips:

*A salad and baked potato make a good
accompaniment. Vegetable oil can be substituted
for corn oil. I usually serve beef and chicken
fondue together with both accompanying sauces.*

PORK & HAM DINNERS

To speak evil of no man, to be no brawlers,
but gentle, shewing all meekness unto all men.

TITUS 3:2

All of us worry and try to protect our children from being physically injured, and that's very important. We want to remove the pain from our loved ones as quickly as possible, but we do not begin to think about how badly we injure each other with our words. When my oldest daughter was around twenty years old, she was all dressed and ready to go out for the evening. She was very skimpily clad, and I was quite upset when I saw her. I suggested that she change her clothes before going out. When she gave me a shrug and implied that I was a prude, I reacted quite badly. I told her in no uncertain terms that she looked like she was a lady of the night. She responded in kind and ran out the door crying. My thoughtless words had hurt her deeply. This wound I inflicted took a lot longer to heal than a cut or skinned knee would take to heal. It took a while for her to forgive me and for me to forgive myself.

God is there to guide you when you need help choosing your words. Never underestimate the power of a word.

Pineapple Ham Loaf

Prepare this meal as an act of forgiveness and reconciliation
for whomever you have offended.

SERVES 6

1 cup (125 grams) bread crumbs

3 eggs

¹/₂ cup (120 milliliters) milk

¹/₂ cup (110 grams) light brown
sugar

2 tablespoons lemon juice

1 teaspoon dry mustard

1 pound (455 grams) lean ground pork

1 pound (455 grams) ground smoked
ham

1 20-ounce (570-milliliter) can sliced
pineapple rings, drained

DIRECTIONS: Combine bread crumbs, eggs, and milk. Stir in sugar
and lemon juice and dry mustard. Add ground meat. Mix thoroughly.
Place mixture in a greased 10" × 10" baking dish, and top with pineapple
rings. Bake at 350°F (180°C) for 80 minutes.

My sister-in-law Gayle shared this recipe with me.

He in the first year of his reign, in the first month,
opened the doors of the house of the LORD,
and repaired them.

2 CHRONICLES 29:3

My daughter was so thrilled when she found a new home. She brought me and her daughter, my granddaughter, over to see the new house before moving in. We took a tour of the house and went upstairs to see the bedrooms. My granddaughter was very excited about her new room. She ran right in and shut the door behind her. My daughter went to the new guestroom and shut the door behind her. The next thing I knew, both of them were twisting and turning the doorknobs of their respective doors, but to no avail. Both doors were jammed shut. "I can't get out!" I heard my granddaughter scream. My daughter yelled, "Mom, help me get out of here!" I went and tried to help both of them, but those doors were stuck shut. My granddaughter began to panic and started screaming and crying. My daughter tried to calm her, but since they were in separate rooms, it wasn't helping. The next thing I knew the next door neighbor came over because he heard screaming. He practically broke down my granddaughter's bedroom door because her pleas were so panicky.

God's door is always open for you. All you have to do is knock.

STUFFED HAM AND CHEESE

Open your door and invite your neighbors
in for some stuffed bread.

MAKES 2 LOAVES

1 package refrigerated Pillsbury
crusty French bread dough

Creamy Dijonnaise

Honey mustard

1 cup (110 grams) grated Swiss cheese,
2 tablespoons (15 grams) reserved
for sprinkling over loaf

½ pound (230 grams) deli ham slices
or shaved ham

1 egg, beaten

DIRECTIONS: On a floured surface, unroll the bread dough. (If bread
is hard to unroll, slice lengthwise and roll out each piece to 4"–6" width.)
Cut in half crosswise, making two pieces. Spread a thin layer of Creamy
Dijonnaise on each half. Squeeze a small amount of honey mustard down
the center of each half. Place folded slices of ham on each half lengthwise.
Place grated cheese over ham. Bring edges together and pinch. Brush
egg on top of bread and sprinkle with cheese. Place on greased baking
sheet, seam side down. Bake at 350°F (180°C) for 20 minutes until
golden brown.

aunt susie's tips:
*These are great for hors d'oeuvres
as well as a main course.*

To know wisdom and instruction; to perceive the words of understanding

PROVERBS 1:2

*C*hildren can be quite perceptive, and they will often state their perceptions in the bluntest of terms. One year our family vacationed in Washington, D.C. My husband, Larry, took our youngest daughter, who was around eight years old at the time, on his visit to the Capitol. They took a tour of the building and, as part of their visit, they went to the visitor's gallery where they were able to observe the legislature in session. As they were sitting there, they watched as the Speaker of the House tried to bring the body of legislators to order. The congressional members seemed to ignore him and kept chatting away with one another, absorbed in what they were doing. One member was even clipping articles from a newspaper. Our daughter watched closely for a while, and then she and Larry left. As they were leaving, Larry asked her what she thought of the legislators. Her response was simply, "I liked them better before I ever saw them."

Children are often God's way of showing us the truth. We should listen to them, for out of the mouths of babes....

PEPPERONI LOAF

Make this pepperoni loaf for some kids you love
—and they'll tell you how good it is.

MAKES 2 LOAVES

1 package refrigerated Pillsbury crusty French bread dough

1/2 pound (225 grams) sliced mild pepperoni

2/3 cup (80 grams) shredded mozzarella cheese

1/4 cup (40 grams) chopped onion

2 tablespoons shredded Asiago cheese

1 egg, beaten

DIRECTIONS: On a floured surface, unroll the bread dough. Cut in half lengthwise. Place pepperoni slices on each half. Top with onions. Place grated mozzarella cheese over pepperoni and onions. Bring edges together and pinch. Brush egg on top of bread and sprinkle with Asiago cheese. Place on greased baking sheet, seam side down. Bake at 350°F (180°C) for 20–25 minutes till golden brown.

aunt susie's tips:
*These are great for hors d'oeuvres
as well as a main course.
I also love to add cooked sausage
when I have more time.*

Blessed be the God and Father of our Lord Jesus Christ, who hath blessed us with all spiritual blessings in heavenly places in Christ.

EPHESIANS 1:3

I have always been a do-it-yourselfer. A few years ago, we were installing a new motion spotlight at the top of our two-story garage. My husband held the ladder for me, and I went up to do the wiring. I put the light up and rewired it, fully expecting it to work. However, when we went to turn the power on to see if the light worked, it did not. Back up the ladder I went to check things out. I took everything apart and put it all back together once again and came back down the ladder. I asked my husband to go turn the power back on so we could see if the light worked. Low and behold, however, when Larry went to turn the power back on, he realized that we had never turned it back off. I was up there at the second story level of my house rewiring a light with the electricity on. Was I ever lucky! I could have been shocked and fallen off the ladder onto the concrete driveway and been hurt very badly or worse. I was very blessed that God was watching over me that day.

God blesses us even in the unexpected moments of our lives. Tell Him how much you appreciate His constant care.

SAUERKRAUT AND RIBS

This is a hearty meal that shows you care about
your family—good tasting and good for you.

SERVES 6 TO 8

2 tablespoons butter

3 packages baby back ribs

Salt and pepper to taste

3 large cans sauerkraut

1 large sweet onion (Vidalia), finely chopped

2 small apples (Gala), finely chopped

$^{1}/_{2}$ cup (120 milliliters) water

DIRECTIONS: In a large, heavy roaster pan, add two tablespoons of butter. Heat and add ribs cut in individual serving sections. Brown on each side, salting and peppering each side as it browns. Remove from roaster. Add three cans of sauerkraut, one at a time, allowing sauerkraut to absorb drippings. Let simmer for five minutes. Add onion and apples, and simmer for another five minutes. Salt and pepper as desired. Return the ribs to roaster, spooning sauerkraut over the meat. Add $^{1}/_{2}$ cup water. Reduce heat to simmer. Cover pan. Check occasionally to make sure there is enough water to keep sauerkraut from burning but not too much water (you don't want to boil the sauerkraut or ribs). Cook until ribs are tender, about $1^{1}/_{2}$ to 2 hours.

My friend Barb shared this recipe with me.

aunt susie's tips:
I add a few tablespoons of sugar to sweeten the sauerkraut a little.

*...us, O LORD our God; for we rest on thee,
and in thy name we go against this multitude.
O LORD, thou art our God; let not man
prevail against thee.*

2 CHRONICLES 14

*O*n our one and only cruise, our ship was taking us to the Greek island of Santorini, a beautiful place. We could not dock there, so we had to take a small boat to get to the island. We were there a couple of hours when the winds became very strong. We decided that it might be a good idea to go back to the ship ahead of schedule. We weren't the only ones with that idea. It seemed like everyone was waiting to get back to the ship. We all waited as the boat attempted to take small groups back to the ship. The water was so choppy and the waves were so high that it took hours. When we finally got onto the boat, we were on the water for an hour, never even getting close to the ship as the seas were too rough. We were taken back to shore. After about six hours of waiting in the cold and rain, we made a second attempt. It was horrific. The waves were so high that I thought the boat was going to capsize, and so did everybody else. There were about eighty of us or so in this small boat, and about a third or more were getting sick. People were crying and panicking, worrying about dying. Those of us who were calm tried to soothe the others by praying together. Finally, we made it to our ship. We were the last ones on board. Some wept as they got onto the ship, happy to be alive.

In times of trouble and shared danger, we can comfort one another by praying together.

PORK BAR-B-Q

Don't forget to thank the Lord with a short prayer
before enjoying this pork Bar-B-Q meal,
perfect when you need to feed a hungry crowd.

MAKES 8

1 1/2–2 pounds (680–910 grams)
  pork loin roast
1/4 cup (60 milliliters) broth from
  cooking pork

1/2 cup (125 grams) barbecue sauce
  (I use Montgomery Inn)
1 cup (240 grams) ketchup
1/2 teaspoon Worcestershire sauce

DIRECTIONS: Put pork in pan and cover with water. Cook on top
of stove for 2 hours or until tender. Drain water, saving 1/4 cup for sauce.
Shred pork with forks or a potato masher. Add broth and remaining
ingredients. Heat and serve on warm buns.

aunt susie's tips:
*I like to serve this open-faced on
a bun, topped with creamy
coleslaw. The pork may also be
cooked in a Crock-Pot.*

...Yea, all of you be subject one to another, and be clothed with humility: for God resisteth the proud, and giveth grace to the humble.

1 PETER 5:5

During the short time I lived in Cincinnati, while I was going to college, among my many experiences was a very humbling one. My sister Marilyn and her husband, Paul, had encouraged me to enter a beauty pageant for tall young women. Since I am five foot ten inches tall, I just qualified for the height limit. I wasn't sure about it, but after much encouragement I decided to give it a try. A seamstress friend of Marilyn's made a beautiful teal blue satin gown for me to wear—I felt like a princess in it. When the big evening came, it was time for me to walk down the beautiful runway. Even though we had practiced walking this runway a few nights before, it still seemed intimidating. I was trying to stay calm despite my excitement and nervousness. As I slowly climbed the steps to the runway, I tripped over my own feet and fell onto the runway. Oh, no! How could I have done this? I quickly picked myself up and made the longest walk of my life.

Accidents can be embarrassing and humbling. Ask God for the grace to help you get through those moments.

BARBECUED RIBS

When you need something fail-proof, serve up these ribs.
Everyone will rave about them.

SERVES 4

2 slabs baby back ribs

1 cup (240 milliliters) water

2 tablespoons barbecue sauce
(I use Montgomery Inn)

1 cup (240 grams) ketchup

1 cup (220 grams) brown sugar

1 tablespoon Worcestershire sauce

DIRECTIONS: Heat oven to 375°F (190°C). Place ribs in pan and add 1 cup water. Cover pan tightly with aluminum foil. Bake for 1 hour. Lay foil aside. Place ribs on foil. Drain water from pan. Put foil back in bottom of pan. Place ribs on foil (this makes for easy cleanup). Combine remaining ingredients and spread over ribs. Cook for an additional 5–10 minutes per side.

aunt susie's tips:

If you like your ribs a little browned and crisp, broil these in the oven for a couple of minutes with the sauce on. Watch them carefully, or they will burn.

Judge not according to the appearance,
but judge righteous judgment.

JOHN 7:24

*D*uring the years when I was running my business, I usually attended at least two candy shows a year in Pennsylvania. We would display our products and offer samples to the many buyers who would come. Before going to one of these shows one year in March, my friend MaryAnn and I were working late and loading the van at around two o'clock in the morning. All of a sudden, there were flashing red lights, a loud siren, and a big spotlight shining right on us. The policeman got out of his car and told us to stop what we were doing. It was pretty unnerving. He asked us for our IDs, and neither one of us had proof of identification with us. We both started talking at once, trying to explain that things are not always as they appear. We weren't stealing things from the store; we were getting ready for a trade show. After about ten minutes of explanations and a phone call to verify our identifications, the policeman left, and we collapsed. We were so shaken up that we quit packing, left the store, and went home. It's so true that appearances can be deceiving.

Sometimes we judge too easily and too harshly without knowing all of the facts. Depend on God to help you avoid these kinds of bad judgments.

PORK TENDERLOIN WITH MUSTARD SAUCE

Fix this and let your guests be the judge of how delicious it is.

SERVES 4 TO 6

1 3-pound (1.4 kilograms) pork tenderloin

1 teaspoon minced garlic

1 teaspoon dried ginger

1/4 cup (60 milliliters) soy sauce

1/2 cup (120 milliliters) bourbon

1/2 cup (110 grams) brown sugar

MUSTARD SAUCE:

1/3 cup (80 grams) sour cream

1/3 cup (80 grams) mayonnaise

1 tablespoon Dijon mustard

1 tablespoon finely chopped scallions

DIRECTIONS: Place tenderloin in a greased 9" × 13" baking dish. Combine remaining ingredients and pour over pork. Marinate several hours or overnight. Bake at 325°F (160°C) for 1 hour. Combine all the ingredients for the Mustard Sauce and chill. Serve with Mustard Sauce.

My friend Sharon shared this recipe with me.

FISH & SEAFOOD

Glory and honour are in his presence;
strength and gladness are in his place.

1 CHRONICLES 16:27

We went on a vacation to Canada and came back to the United States by way of Niagara Falls, being able to see it both on the Canadian side and the American side. How awesome! How spectacular! It was almost too much for the senses. It was over-powering. I have never felt God's presence so much as I did when we were in the Cave of the Winds at Niagara Falls. I cannot begin to tell you what a strong and overpowering feeling it was. As I am growing older, I am finally beginning to appreciate the beauty of nature and God's presence in all this beauty. Just watching the sunset or seeing the sky full of stars or the snow falling in big flakes on the bare trees in the dead of winter can make you feel so close to God. Feeling God's presence everywhere and developing a deeper appreciation of nature has been a true gift, one available to each one of us every day of our lives. Look out your window in the morning. Feel the joy of being alive and seeing all that nature has to hold.

Don't let a day escape you without stopping to appreciate the glory of our world.

CRAB LEGS

These crab legs will make you thankful
for God's glories of the sea.

SERVES 4

—◦◦◦—

2–3 pounds (1–1.4 kilograms) king crab or snow crab legs
Butter
Lemon wedges

DIRECTIONS: Fill a pot large enough to hold the crab legs with
water. Bring water to boil. Drop 2–3 pounds of king crab or snow
crab legs into the pot for 3–5 minutes until hot. Drain well. Serve
with melted butter and lemon wedges. Really good and very simple.

My sister Marilyn shared this recipe with me.

Be ye strong therefore, and let not your hands be
weak: for your work shall be rewarded.

2 CHRONICLES 15:7

I have heard it said that when we stop making mistakes, we are no
longer alive. When my partner and I were operating our popcorn
store, we had been cleaning the store ourselves, so we hired a young
man to clean the store for us. It was wonderful to have this young man
help relieve us of some of the work. One evening I went to check on
him. He was so excited to see me. He had been working very hard. He
said he wanted to show me something he had been working on, and he
ran over to the sink. He brought the popcorn baller over and opened
it up. He pointed to one side of it and said, "See the dirty side? Now
look how clean the other side is. Look how well I cleaned it up." I
looked at him and didn't know quite what to say. This young man had
apparently scrubbed and scrubbed, removing the Teflon coating on one
side of the popcorn baller, thinking that the Teflon coating was just dirt.
He left one side with the Teflon coating on to show me how dirty it had
been and how clean the other one was. The popcorn baller was ruined.
It was a fairly costly piece of equipment, but the money did not seem to
matter. This young man was so proud of his effort, and I admired him
for that. I told him about the coating, and did my best to make him
laugh, and pretty soon we were both laughing about it together.

*Our ability to laugh at our mishaps is a sign of strength and not weak-
ness. God gave us a sense of humor. Be sure to use it.*

SWORDFISH & PINEAPPLE SALSA

Prepare this snazzy salsa swordfish,
and you'll be rewarded with your guests' pleasure.

SERVES 4

———⁂———

4 swordfish fillets

2 teaspoons soy sauce mixed with
1 teaspoon sugar

PINEAPPLE SALSA:

$1/2$ teaspoon minced garlic

1 diced tomato

1 8-ounce (235-milliliter) can
pineapple tidbits, drained

1 teaspoon cilantro

$1/4$ teaspoon lime juice

$1/2$ teaspoon sugar

DIRECTIONS: Place swordfish on greased broiler pan. Brush swordfish with soy sauce and sugar mixture. Broil in oven for 5–7 minutes,
turning once. Fish is ready when it flakes easily with a fork. To make
pineapple salsa, mix all ingredients in medium bowl. Serve swordfish
with pineapple salsa.

And when Saul saw the host of the Philistines,
he was afraid, and his heart greatly trembled.

1 SAMUEL 28:5

A number of years ago I decided to try my hand as a tax preparer. I had just finished my courses and was anxious to begin. I was going to work part time so I could still be home when my children came home from school. My stint, however, didn't last too long. After I had been working for about three weeks, a man in his late seventies came in and needed his taxes prepared. As I was doing my job, he kept saying to me, "You better do my taxes right, or I'm going to kill you." He kept saying it over and over, and then he added, "and I know just how to do it." With that, he pulled a knife out of his pocket, pointed it right at me, and said, "Feel how sharp that blade is." I was so scared that I wanted to scream. Instead, I said calmly, "Now put that thing away. You're going to hurt yourself." I finally persuaded him to put it away, appearing calm but feeling like jelly on the inside. I continued to finish his taxes. In a way I felt sorry for this senile old man, but I was terrified. When I finished, I stood up and hurriedly ushered him out of the store.

When you find yourself in fear, do as I did—call upon the Lord once again for His much-needed help.

Flounder with Veggies

Fear not—dinner will be ready in a jiffy with this quick recipe.

Serves 4

—◊◊◊—

2 pounds (910 grams) flounder
2 zucchini
2 yellow squash

2 portobello mushrooms, sliced
Italian dressing

DIRECTIONS: Preheat oven to broil. Spray broiler pan with nonstick cooking spray. Slice zucchini and squash lengthwise into about 4–6 slices. Place fish and vegetables on broiler pan. Brush fish and vegetables with Italian dressing. Broil for about 5–8 minutes. Serve immediately.

aunt susie's tips:
You could also use ranch dressing for a different taste.

One of his disciples, Andrew, Simon Peter's brother, saith unto him, There is a lad here, which hath five barley loaves, and two small fishes: but what are they among so many?

JOHN 6:8–9

The story of the multiplying of the bread and fish reminds me of a time when I needed such a miracle. It happened that a friend of mine who ran her own home catering business was in desperate need of help. She had promised to cater a wedding on Saturday, but on the Wednesday afternoon before, her son was severely injured in an accident and in serious condition in the hospital. She called and asked me if I could possibly cater the wedding. What could I say? After she gave me the menu to be served, I ran to the grocery and called my friends for much-needed help. It was a bit frenzied, but thanks to all, the food was ready! Saturday came all too soon, and we went to the reception hall and set up for the hungry wedding party and guests that were soon to come. But, instead of the 150 guests expected, there were almost 200! Hurriedly, we cut the remaining stuffed mushrooms in half, quartered the finger sandwiches, broke the bread into smaller pieces, and added more mayonnaise and sour cream to the spinach dip. Afterwards, I thanked my friends and my guardian angel for the much-needed help and for helping me keep my composure.

There are many people in our country without enough food to eat. Make a food donation to your local shelter.

CRUSTY SALMON

If you have unexpected dinner guests, you can easily stretch this recipe.

SERVES 4

1 11-ounce (310-gram) package Pillsbury Crusty French Loaf

4 4–6-ounce (115–170-gram) salmon fillets, with skin removed

1 10-ounce (285-gram) package frozen spinach, thawed and well drained

²/₃ cup (80 grams) shredded mozzarella cheese

²/₃ cup (80 grams) grated Parmesan cheese

¹/₄ cup (60 grams) Dijonnaise

Vegetable oil spray

DIRECTIONS: Preheat oven to 350°F (180°C). On a floured surface, unroll the French bread into a rectangle and stretch a little bit (it is in a roll, so it is quick and easy to unroll). Cut the dough into four even pieces. Put one salmon fillet onto each piece of dough. Squeeze spinach to remove any remaining liquid. Spread 1 tablespoon of Dijonnaise on top of salmon fillet. Put ¹/₄ package of spinach on each fillet. Mix mozzarella and Parmesan cheeses together. Put ¹/₃ cup (40 grams) shredded cheese over spinach. Pinch dough together on all four sides. Spray vegetable oil on cookie sheet. Put the salmon bundles on the tray. Bake for 22–28 minutes. Serve this with salad, and dinner is on. Yum!

aunt susie's tips:

I love to fix this recipe because it is not only delicious, but it is also quick and easy, and this recipe can be prepared for more people if you make your bundles smaller.

Honour thy father and thy mother:
that thy days may be long upon the land
which the LORD thy God giveth thee.

EXODUS 20:12

*J*udy just turned ninety-two and is just starting to get a little
weak. She has battled cancer three times and won, and she has
also had Crohn's disease for the last twenty years. However, she is still
on the go, doing volunteer work and being active in the assisted living
area where she now lives. She has always concentrated on giving to
others instead of thinking of herself. When she was in her eighties,
she seemed like a woman of sixty. She is an inspiration to all those
who are going into the golden years of their lives.

All of us want to live a long and healthy life. Ask God to bless you with
this and use this life to help others.

Salmon Teriyaki

Salmon boasts anti-aging qualities.
Cook up this healthy meal for your elderly loved ones.

Serves 4

½ cup (120 milliliters) orange juice

⅓ cup (80 milliliters) soy sauce

6 tablespoons honey

½ teaspoon ginger

1 teaspoon garlic powder

2 teaspoons minced onion

4 6–8-ounce (170–230-gram) salmon fillets

DIRECTIONS: In a bowl, combine the first six ingredients. Mix well. Coat salmon on both sides with mixture; reserve remaining marinade. Cook fillets in skillet over medium-high heat. Turn over at least once. When fillets are nearly done, pour the rest of the sauce over the fillets. Continue cooking for about 3 more minutes.

...We trust in the LORD our God...

2 KINGS 18:22

My children are avid animal lovers, particularly of dogs and cats. I wish I could say they inherited this deep feeling and concern for animals from their father or me. I have always been afraid of animals to a certain extent, at least until I can really get to know them. One day out of the blue, our daughter brought home a dog, and of course she wanted to keep her. I was a little leery, but since our last dog had died, the kids were missing having a family dog. Madison was housetrained, but she started barking when we came near her, and I was a little bit afraid. In time, she became protective of everyone in the family, and she was a wonderful, loving dog. I overcame my fear of her as we learned to trust each other. The one thing we had to be careful of, however, was leaving food on the table. She loved to eat. One evening I left the kitchen to call everyone to dinner, but when they came in, the dinner on the table was gone. The dog had climbed up on the table and eaten all of the fried chicken, bones and all. She was also very fond of these tuna burgers.

God places His trust in us all the time. Place your trust in Him today— and His creatures, that bring such love into our lives.

TUNA BURGERS

You can trust that your family will love this dish;
share a tidbit with your cat or dog as well.

MAKES 12

4 6-ounce (175-milliliter) cans of
water-packed tuna, drained

1 small can sliced green olives

¼ cup (60 grams) Miracle Whip or
mayonnaise

1 small onion, minced

1 8-ounce (230-gram) package of
shredded cheddar cheese

12 hamburger buns

Butter or margarine

DIRECTIONS: Combine all ingredients except buns and butter in a
bowl. Butter both tops and bottoms of hamburger buns, and place a large
spoonful of tuna mixture on bottom half of each bun. Place tops on buns
and wrap in aluminum foil. Bake at 350°F (180°C) for 20–30 minutes.

My friend and neighbor Jim shared this recipe with me.

PASTA

But the stranger that dwelleth with you shall be unto you as one born among you, and thou shalt love him as thyself; for ye were strangers in the land of Egypt: I am the LORD your God.

LEVITICUS 19:34

How many of us have read Dr. Seuss's books about the Sneetches to our children? It is a cute, silly story teaching our children, and us, too, a valuable lesson. I was fortunate enough to be raised in a home where my parents taught us that all of us are God's people and are in this world together, and we need each other's help in getting through this world. When I was in college, I got my first taste of intolerance. A good friend and I were out to lunch one day when she started making bigoted comments about another good friend of mine who happened to be Jewish. I couldn't believe I was hearing this from the friend I thought I knew so well. I was very offended by the comments she was making and told her so. We got into a rather heated discussion, and I ended up leaving the restaurant, unable to tolerate her ignorance. Why do people carry on their prejudices? We should do our best to treat each other well while we are here and speak out against prejudice whenever the opportunity arises.

God wants us all to live by the Golden Rule. As the saying goes, "Treat others as you would like to be treated."

CHICKEN PASTA

Surprise a friend who's suffered an injustice
with this lovely chicken dish.

SERVES 6 TO 8

8 ounces (230 grams) angel hair pasta

2 cups (280 grams) cooked chicken
breast, cut into bite-sized pieces

1 10-ounce (280-gram) can cream of
chicken soup

1 10-ounce (280-gram) can cream of
mushroom soup

¾ cup (180 milliliters) milk

¼ cup (30 grams) shredded Asiago
cheese

¼ cup (30 grams) shredded
Parmesan cheese

¼ teaspoon hot sauce, optional

DIRECTIONS: Cook pasta according to package directions. While pasta
is cooking, combine remaining ingredients, mixing well. Drain pasta. Toss
pasta, chicken, and soup mixture all together. Put into a greased 9" × 13"
pan. Bake at 350°F (180°C) for 25–35 minutes.

My sister Marilyn shared this recipe with me.

aunt susie's tips:

*I always use angel hair pasta because it cooks faster. You can also
substitute ¼ cup (60 milliliters) white wine for part of the milk
for a great taste. Try adding some spinach for another great taste.*

A gift is as a precious stone in the eyes of him that hath it: whithersoever it turneth, it prospereth.

PROVERBS 17:8

C hristmas is a hectic time at our house with all the decorating, cooking, and shopping that goes with the season. And, of course, there are so many things to be done at the last minute that you hadn't planned. Sometimes the fun becomes work as you keep looking for the right gift to give. One of my friends was very hard to shop for. She seemed to have everything. I spent hours trying to find a gift I thought she would really enjoy. I searched and searched and finally found a beautiful Christmas ornament for her. I went to her home (I hadn't seen her for quite some time), and she was as thrilled to see me as I was to see her. I knew I should have been home finishing my Christmas preparations, but we were having such a wonderful time catching up on each other's lives. As I finally left to go home, she thanked me for the ornament and then added, "Having you come and visit with me was the best gift of all." Here I had searched and searched for the perfect gift, and all the time it was right there where I couldn't see it.

The gifts of God are all around us and cannot be bought. All you have to do is look around and appreciate them.

CHICKEN AND NOODLES

This is the perfect winter stand-by for guests, expected and unexpected, in those busy, bustling days during the holiday rush.

SERVES 4 TO 6

8–10 cups (1.9–2.4 liters) chicken broth

1 8-ounce (230-gram) package medium noodles

1 teaspoon garlic powder

1 teaspoon onion powder

½ teaspoon poultry seasoning, optional

1 teaspoon sage

4–6 cooked chicken breasts, cut into bite-sized pieces

3 tablespoons flour

½ cup (120 milliliters) milk

DIRECTIONS: In a large pot, bring chicken broth to a boil and add noodles. Cook noodles according to directions on package. Do not drain. Add seasonings and chicken. In a small cup, mix flour and milk together until smooth. Add gradually to boiling chicken and noodles to thicken to desired consistency. Reduce heat and serve.

aunt susie's tips:

This is great served over mashed potatoes. I love to use Inn Maid Kluski noodles for this recipe.

But they were terrified and affrighted,
and supposed that they had seen a spirit.

LUKE 24:37

*A*re you one of those people who startles easily? I certainly am. Maybe it's because I'm so absorbed with what I'm doing. My being startled easily and screaming loudly when I am startled has become a source of amusement for my children and some of my nieces and nephews. They look for opportune times to scare me, and when I yell, they laugh and laugh. They also like to play practical jokes on me. On one occasion, I was driving to Indiana to see my sister one evening, and it was just around dusk. I was all by myself, driving on a state highway. As I was getting close to my sister's house, I noticed the same car had been closely following me for quite a few miles. From the inside of the car, a red light started flashing. Who could be following me? Was this a policeman in an unmarked car? I was traveling under the speed limit, so I couldn't imagine what I could be doing wrong. All of a sudden, the car started blinking its lights on and off. What was I going to do? I was a wreck. After a few minutes, I decided that I had better pull over. Then the car behind me pulled over as well and I saw someone step out of his car and approach my car. I rolled down the window just a little, keeping my doors locked, and tried to keep calm. Then when he said, "May I see your license?" I thought his voice sounded familiar. I looked up, and there he was: my nephew, grinning from ear to ear. I said, "You stinker. Do you know how scared I was?" We both started laughing.

Often our fears are unfounded—let God help you learn to laugh at your little phobias, along with your children.

Spaghetti Red

Kids love this simple, but tasty spaghetti. Serve it up
the next time you watch a scary movie together.

Serves 4

8 ounces (230 grams) angel hair pasta
1 32-ounce (910-gram) jar red pasta sauce
Grated Parmesan cheese

DIRECTIONS: Prepare pasta according to directions on package. Heat
sauce until warm. Drain pasta well and put back in pan. Add sauce and
toss until well mixed. Serve immediately with cheese.

My friend David shared this recipe with me.

aunt susie's tips:
*If you don't have grated Parmesan,
you can use any kind of finely
shredded white cheese.*

And now, behold, the LORD
hath kept me alive…

JOSHUA 14:10

In September 1993, my husband, Larry, had to have an angio-plasty. The angioplasty went well, and he was ready to come home an hour after it was done. Luckily, they insisted on keeping him overnight. I stayed for a few hours and then went home, leaving him in good spirits. As soon as I got home, I got on my pajamas and hopped into bed. As my head hit the pillow, the phone rang. It was the hospital, telling me to get there immediately. Larry had sneezed, and the clamp on his femoral artery (on his thigh) had come undone. They couldn't get it back on. He lost a great deal of blood and had a major heart attack. They defibrillated him ten times and finally revived him. When I arrived at the hospital, they were taking him to surgery for a heart bypass. The healthy man I had seen hours before looked so pale and gray. Fortunately, he made it through the surgery in great shape. Today he is in good health. This certainly brought home to us the fact that life can change in an instant.

The gift of life has been bestowed upon us by a loving God. Thank Him for this gift each and every day.

CHICKEN LASAGNA

This lasagna is the perfect casserole to present to ailing friends
or those with loved ones in the hospital.

SERVES 6 TO 8

1 8-ounce (230-gram) package cream cheese

1 10-ounce (280-gram) can cream of mushroom soup

Dash salt

Dash pepper

1 teaspoon (3 grams) minced onion

1 package oven-ready lasagna noodles

6 cooked chicken breasts, cut into bite-sized pieces

1 16-ounce (450-gram) container cottage cheese

1 8-ounce (230-gram) package mozzarella slices

1 8-ounce (230-gram) package provolone slices

DIRECTIONS: In saucepan, warm cream cheese and soup at medium heat and stir. Add salt, pepper, and minced onion. Remove from heat. Place a layer of lasagna noodles over bottom of lasagna pan or 9" × 13" pan. On top of the noodles, layer half of the chicken, then half of the cottage cheese, and finally half of the soup/cream cheese mixture in even layers. Layer with half the mozzarella slices and half the provolone slices. Place another layer of lasagna noodles, remaining chicken, cottage cheese, and soup/cream cheese mixture. Cover evenly with remaining cheese. Bake at 350°F (180°C) for 30–45 minutes or until it is golden brown and bubbly.

My friend and neighbor Melanie shared this recipe with me.

VEGETABLE & SIDE DISHES

To the end that my glory may sing praise to thee, and not be silent. O LORD my God, I will give thanks unto thee forever.

PSALM 30:12

At the time of my mother's death, I was a student in high school and had to move in with my older sister Anita, her husband Jim, and their three children (and another child was on the way). They had a little house with three bedrooms and, lucky for me, a basement. I moved into the basement with a few of my possessions, and that was my home for the next year. Being a teenager at the time, I was very self-centered, and I didn't think of the impact my moving in with Anita and her family would have on their lives. I was busy feeling sorry for myself, losing both Mom and Dad within five months of each other. Today I look back and wonder how they managed to cope. They were just in their mid-thirties. She and her husband Jim were very good to me and treated me like one of their own children. I'm not sure she knows how very much I appreciated her mothering, her sistering, and the many sacrifices she and her husband made to care for me.

How many times do we forget to thank those who are good to us and acknowledge them as God's blessings in our lives? Thank a loved one today.

SCALLOPED PINEAPPLE

This pineapple bread pudding makes a lovely
thank-you for a loved one.

SERVES 8 TO 10

6 cups (210 grams) soft bread cubes

¾ cup (180 milliliters) milk

1 stick margarine, melted

1½ cups (300 grams) sugar

3 eggs

1 20-ounce (570-milliliter) can
crushed pineapple, drained

DIRECTIONS: In a large bowl, moisten bread cubes with the milk.
Add remaining ingredients, mixing well. Pour into a greased 9" × 13" pan.
Bake at 350°F (180°C) for 30–35 minutes.

My sister Anita shared this recipe with me.

aunt susie's tips:
*Have cinnamon sugar handy as
some, like myself, love it on this!*

And I myself also am persuaded of you,
my brethren, that ye also are full of goodness…

ROMANS 15:14

"*S*isters, sisters, there were never such devoted sisters." When my three sisters and I get together, we break into song, singing "Sisters." Oh, what a kick! Since my sisters and I live in different states, the phone has become a necessity. I love to call my sisters and see what's going on and also find out what I'm missing by not being around them. Maybe it's because I'm the youngest of the group, but I'm glad it's so easy to "reach out and touch" my sisters. We manage to get together a couple of times a year. My sisters had to take on the role of my parents for a while since my mom and dad died at such an early age. It was a dirty job, but somebody had to do it, and a good job they did. But now since I'm older and wiser (I hope), we've been great friends as well as sisters.

Cherish the goodness of your God-given siblings. Call your brother or sister today.

CHEESY POTATOES

This hearty potato dish is perfect for family
potluck get-togethers.

SERVES 8

2 packages instant mashed potatoes,
prepared according to package
instructions, excluding the salt

3 eggs

½ cup (60 grams) grated Parmesan
or Italian mix shredded cheese

3 tablespoons chopped parsley

Salt and pepper to taste

1 8-ounce (230-gram) package
mozzarella slices

1 8-ounce (230-gram) package
provolone slices

DIRECTIONS: Preheat oven to 350°F (180°C). Place prepared mashed potatoes into large bowl. Add one egg at a time and beat well. Stir in Parmesan cheese, parsley, salt, and pepper. Spray a 2-quart casserole with nonstick cooking spray. Fill casserole with alternate layers of potato mixture and a combination of sliced mozzarella and sliced provolone cheese. Bake 45 minutes to 1 hour or until the top is golden and the edges begin to shrink away from the dish.

aunt susie's tips:

*I make this a day ahead of time and refrigerate. Then let it stand
an hour at room temperature before baking. This works well.*

And be renewed in the spirit of your mind.

EPHESIANS 4:23

About ten years ago, I went to a wonderful retreat with a friend of mine. I had never been to a retreat before and didn't know how I was going to like it. Both of us needed some time to rest and renew our spiritual and mental health. We keep on going like the Energizer Bunny, and there are times when we need to recharge our batteries. On our weekend retreat, we received a much-needed rest while examining our lives in all aspects. We rededicated ourselves to the Lord and renewed ourselves spiritually as well. The retreat has helped me in my daily life in many ways. It has helped me to try and imitate Christ's example in my everyday life and to treat others as he would have treated them, which is not an easy thing to do.

Go on a retreat with your religious group. Or organize your own with a few spiritually-minded companions. It will renew your faith and refresh your soul.

SWEET POTATO CASSEROLE

This rich but homey casserole is a retreat favorite.

SERVES 6 TO 8

3 tablespoons butter or margarine

1 cup (200 grams) sugar

1 egg

$^1\!/_2$ cup (120 milliliters) milk

1 teaspoon vanilla

1 large can or 3 small cans sweet
potatoes or yams, drained

TOPPING:

2 tablespoons butter or margarine

1 cup (220 grams) brown sugar

1 tablespoon flour

$^3\!/_4$ cup (90 grams) pecans

DIRECTIONS: Melt butter in pan over medium heat. Add sugar, egg, milk, and vanilla. Add sweet potatoes or yams and beat with mixer until smooth. Pour mixture into a greased 9" × 11" pan. Combine topping ingredients and sprinkle evenly over mixture. Bake at 350°F (180°C) for 30–45 minutes or until top bubbles.

My daughter Stacey shared this recipe with me.

And thou shalt anoint them, as thou didst anoint their father, that they may minister unto me in the priest's office: for their anointing shall surely be an everlasting priesthood throughout their generations.

EXODUS 40:15

M y first meeting with Father George was definitely a memorable one. He was coming to have dinner with my sister Marilyn, her husband, Paul, their daughter Paula, and me. When he first arrived, Paul was not yet home. As we invited Father George inside, Paul's dog (a large, intimidating, protective weimaraner) started barking loudly and tried to jump the small gate that kept him inside their family room. Marilyn, my sister, could not get him to calm down. We all thought he would jump the gate or break it down. As it was in the cold of winter, Marilyn, Paula, Father George, and I had to go upstairs and shut ourselves in the laundry room. It seemed forever until Paul came home and took control of the dog.

Father George just recently turned seventy-five, and we have all appreciated his wonderful friendship over the years. This dedicated and devoted man has touched the lives of so many people throughout his fifty-plus years as a priest.

God has given us dedicated spiritual leaders to take care of his flocks. Appreciate those who enrich your spiritual life.

———◦◦◦———

VEGETABLE QUICHE

Surprise your favorite clergy with this Sunday morning favorite.

SERVES 6

—∞∞—

1 package frozen cauliflower, broccoli, and carrots (or any mixture you prefer), thawed

$\frac{1}{3}$ cup (50 grams) chopped onion

$\frac{1}{2}$ teaspoon onion powder

$\frac{1}{2}$ teaspoon garlic powder

$1\frac{1}{2}$ cups (175 grams) shredded cheese

$1\frac{1}{2}$ cups (360 milliliters) milk

$\frac{2}{3}$ cup (80 grams) Bisquick

3 eggs

DIRECTIONS: Spray a 9" or 10" pie plate with nonstick cooking spray. Mix vegetables, onion, onion powder, garlic powder, and cheese in pie plate. Beat milk, Bisquick, and eggs until smooth. Pour over mixture in pie plate. Bake until golden brown at 375–400°F (190–200°C) for 40 minutes to 1 hour.

My sister-in-law Gayle shared this recipe with me.

aunt susie's tips:
Sausage, ham, or bacon can be added for a variation. This could be a main dish for dinner or a breakfast dish in the morning.

...What shall I do for thee?...

2 KINGS 4:2

*H*ow many times have your children awakened you in the middle of the night, asking for your help? One such night I was sleeping soundly and was awakened by my daughter. She was crying, and I couldn't quite understand what she was saying except that she needed help. She had just moved back home and was setting up her bedroom in the basement. She grabbed my arm and led me to the basement. I followed her in a sleepy haze. As I walked down the basement stairs, I heard the sound of running water. There, in the middle of the basement, was what looked like a giant marshmallow with water sprouting from the middle. My daughter had fallen asleep on the chair while filling her waterbed, and the water kept filling the mattress and expanding it to about three times its size. The hose had eventually popped out, spraying her with water and waking her up to this unbelievable scene. I just started laughing, thanking God profusely that it was in the basement and not on the top level of our home.

God's little children often need comforting in the middle of the night. Ask God to help you to always be there for them.

MASHED POTATOES
WITH CHEESE

Mashed potatoes are the ultimate comfort food—share these
along with your heart with a frightened child.

SERVES 6 TO 8

1 cup (115 grams) shredded cheddar
cheese
1 cup (115 grams) shredded Monterey
Jack cheese

1 cup (230 grams) sour cream
Instant mashed potatoes prepared
for 8 servings
4 tablespoons butter

DIRECTIONS: Add cheeses and sour cream to prepared potatoes and
stir together. Pour into a greased 9" × 9" baking dish. Cut butter into
tablespoon sections. Press pats of butter gently into potatoes, one in each
corner. Bake for approximately 45 minutes at 350°F (180°C) or until
golden brown.

My daughter Stacey shared this recipe with me.

Get wisdom, get understanding; forget it not;
neither decline from the words of my mouth.
Forsake her not, and she shall preserve thee:
love her, and she shall keep thee.

PROVERBS 4:5–6

As a young mother, I had a lot to learn. My son was a bit of a difficult child in his younger years and was prone to temper tantrums. I remember one particular day when he was around three years old. We were in church, seated in a pew in one of the front rows. As we were waiting for the priest to walk up the aisle to the altar, my son was beginning to misbehave. I tried to quiet him down before the mass started. As the priest started his walk up the aisle, my son started getting very loud and belligerent. I tried as hard as I could to pick him up so that we could leave and not disturb the mass. As the priest came closer, he could not help but see what was going on. He stopped outside our row, looked down at me, motioned with the sign of the cross, and said, "Bless you, my child." He walked away, and I left with my upset son, very embarrassed and self-conscious. I learned in time how to calm my son down as well as another very important lesson: Always sit near the back of the church.

Ask God for the wisdom to help get you through difficult situations.

BROCCOLI CASSEROLE

**Broccoli is brain food—and even kids will eat it
when it's prepared this way.**

SERVES 8

½ cup (80 grams) chopped onion

4 tablespoons butter or margarine

¼ cup (60 milliliters) milk

¼ cup (60 milliliters) water

½ pound (225 grams) Velveeta
cheese, cubed

2 10-ounce (285-gram) packages
frozen chopped broccoli, thawed

3 eggs, well beaten

¼ cup (30 grams) breadcrumbs

2 tablespoons butter or margarine,
melted

DIRECTIONS: Sauté onion in 4 tablespoons butter. Add milk and
water, stirring until mixture comes to a boil. Add cheese and stir in until
melted. Add broccoli and eggs, stirring well. Pour into a greased 2-quart
casserole dish. Top with breadcrumbs mixed with 2 tablespoons melted
butter. Bake at 325°F (160°C) for 30 minutes.

*For God is not the author of confusion,
but of peace...*

I CORINTHIANS 14:33

*S*ome days it seems that everything goes wrong. One particular day, I was answering phones at my husband's office while the office staff was at an off-site seminar for a week. I decided his office needed a good cleaning. First I tried to wash the windows, deciding that I needed to take them out for a good cleaning. While trying to put them back in, one window jammed and would not budge. It was half in and half out. I hurried and found one of the men who was painting in the building to help me. After thirty minutes, he finally fixed the window. Undaunted by the experience with the window, I ventured into another area. I had brought a can of stain in with me to touch up my husband's office furniture. I accidentally spilled the stain all over the rug. I had visions of having to buy new carpet for his office, costing thousands of dollars. After using two gallons of paint remover and about six hours of hard labor, the rug was almost like new. Out of a day of chaos and confusion finally came some order—thanks to the Lord and some hard work.

There are times when we need God to bring order to our chaos and confusion. Ask Him to do so for you.

CORN CAKE

This sweet corn cake recipe is not to be
confused with corn bread.

SERVES 4 TO 6

1 8.5-ounce (240-gram) package
corn bread mix

1 small can creamed corn

½ cup (100 grams) sugar

1 teaspoon vanilla

1 egg

DIRECTIONS: Prepare corn bread mix according to directions on
package. Add remaining ingredients and stir together. Pour into greased
baking dish and bake at 375°F (190°C) for 30–45 minutes.

*But it is good to be zealously affected always
in a good thing, and not only when
I am present with you.*

GALATIANS 4:18

How many of you remember Donna Reed, June Cleaver, and "Mrs. Father Knows Best"? They remind me a lot of my mother. So, my ambition was to be just like my mom, Donna, June, and "Mrs. Father Knows Best." I wanted at least four children like my mom had, and I was so excited about growing up and becoming just like Mom. After my parents died when I was still a teenager, my environment completely changed. I still longed for the family in which I grew up. This, I think, increased my desire even more to get married and have children and be a mom like my mother. My ambition became a reality, but being a mother took on a whole new meaning. Motherhood is a real job and one that has no end. I still call on my mom in heaven to help me out down here. My children have brought much joy into my life and helped me grow as a person. I may not be the mom my mother was, but I did reach my goal, and what a journey it has been.

Thank God for the terrific role models in your life. Say thank you to your mom today, in person or in prayer.

POTATO LEGS

These quick and easy appetizers are considered
good things with Moms and kids alike.

SERVES 4 TO 6

————≈————

5 medium baking potatoes

1 8-ounce (230-gram) package
shredded cheddar cheese

2 tablespoons butter
or margarine, melted

Sour cream

DIRECTIONS: Wash potatoes and cut lengthwise into wedges. Place potatoes into a greased 9" × 9" baking dish. Brush potatoes with butter. Cover pan with aluminum foil. Bake for 45–60 minutes at 350°F (180°C). Remove from oven and cover potatoes with cheese. Dollop with sour cream.

My friend and neighbor April shared this recipe with me.

And we have sent with them our brother,
whom we have oftentimes proved diligent in
many things, but now much more diligent, upon
the great confidence which I have in you.

2 CORINTHIANS 8:22

Alaskan malamutes are my son's obsession. When he was living at home, he went out and bought an Alaskan malamute puppy, and he named her Jeannie. He decided to live in the unfinished basement with her while she was still young so that he could care for her. He bought a huge kennel for her about ten feet by eight feet by five feet high, and he set it up in the basement. This little puppy grew into a big puppy in only a few months. One day I went downstairs and found her sitting on the bed. I thought I had forgotten to lock her in the kennel cage. (We had to keep her in the cage as she was chewing everything in sight and had not yet been housebroken.) I put her in the cage and went back upstairs. I walked back downstairs a little bit later, and there she was, roaming around again. She had gotten a pillow and had torn it to shreds. I couldn't figure it out. I locked her up once more and went back upstairs. Then I sneaked back down to find this clever, agile dog climbing the cage. So, we had to build the cage higher—it looked like a maximum-security prison, but we kept her in. Talk about persistence. Jeannie was one diligent, determined dog.

When you feel like giving up—don't. Ask God to instill you with the
diligence you need to keep on going.

HASHBROWN CASSEROLE

Reward your diligence during the work week with this
delicious breakfast casserole on Sunday morning.
Serve with scrambled eggs and fruit.

SERVES 8 TO 10

- 1 32-ounce (910-gram) bag frozen hash browns
- 1 stick of butter or margarine, melted
- 1 pint (460 grams) sour cream
- 1 10-ounce (280-gram) can cream of chicken soup
- ¼ cup (25 grams) chopped green onion
- 12 ounces (340 grams) shredded cheese

DIRECTIONS: Mix all ingredients and pour into a greased 9" × 13" baking dish. Bake at 350°F (180°C) for about 20–30 minutes.

My friend and niece Joan shared this recipe with me.

aunt susie's tips:
When I make this recipe, I use 1½–2 cans cream of chicken soup and 3 cups (345 grams) shredded cheese. I also bake it longer, usually 30–45 minutes.

...God hath made me to laugh, so that all that hear will laugh with me.

GENESIS 21:6

We called Athens, Georgia, our home for about six months when my husband attended the Navy Supply Corp. School in this lovely college community. We lived in a small apartment near my sister Marilyn and her family. It was so much fun living so close to each other. Once we went into town to do some shopping. We were looking for a parking space and saw one by a jewelry store. The parking places were diagonal, so you didn't have to worry about parallel parking. My sister started to pull into the parking spot. As she came to a stop, she accidentally hit the accelerator and knocked down the parking meter. She immediately hit the brakes, and we came to a halting stop. The people in the jewelry store had run to the front of the store and were glaring at us with big eyes. We wanted to disappear, but when we saw that no one was hurt and we had only bent the parking meter, we started laughing uncontrollably.

Laughter is one of God's greatest gifts to us. Use this gift daily. Laughter truly is the best medicine.

TATER TOT CASSEROLE

This silly-sounding potato dish makes
kids of all ages laugh—and eat up.

SERVES 8 TO 10

2 pounds (910 grams) frozen potato
nuggets

1 8-ounce (230-gram) package
shredded Co-Jack cheese

2 10-ounce (280-gram) cans cream
of celery soup

$^1/_2$ cup (115 grams) sour cream

$^1/_2$ stick butter or margarine, melted

2 tablespoons bacon bits

$^1/_2$ cup (120 milliliters) milk

DIRECTIONS: In a greased 9" × 13" pan, mash potato nuggets. Mix
remaining ingredients, pour over potato nuggets. Cook at 350°F (180°C)
for 30–40 minutes.

My friend and neighbor Celia shared this recipe with me.

aunt susie's tips:
*Real bacon bits are now available in
jars at your grocer's. I found them in
the aisle with the condiments.*

DESSERTS
& SWEETS

...The LORD, before whom I walk, will send his angel with thee, and prosper thy way...

GENESIS 24:40

Being educated in the Catholic school system back in the late 1940s and 1950s, we learned a lot about angels. We were taught that each one of us has our own guardian angel. She was always with us to watch over us, protect us, and keep us out of harm's way. And, of course, I loved my guardian angel around and always wanted her with me. Well, my three older sisters used to love to tease me and get me to cry. They used to say, "Uh-oh, Susie, you've been naughty. There goes your guardian angel running down the alley." Then I'd start crying and run out the door and down the alley and yell for my guardian angel to come back. Today I still believe my guardian angel is with me and has helped me through good times and bad times.

What would we do without our angels? God's angels come in all forms. Be sure to recognize them when you see them.

FOAM PIE

This is a heavenly dessert as light as an angel's wing.

SERVES 6 TO 8

1 8-ounce (230-gram) package
cream cheese, softened

1 14-ounce (415-milliliter) can
sweetened condensed milk

2 teaspoons vanilla

⅓ cup (80 milliliters) lime juice

1 9-ounce (255-gram) prepared
graham cracker crust

1 8-ounce (230-gram) container
frozen whipped topping, thawed

DIRECTIONS: Beat cream cheese till smooth. Add sweetened condensed milk, vanilla, and lime juice and beat together. Pour mixture into prepared crust. Spread whipped topping evenly over top. Refrigerate until time to serve.

My sister Marilyn shared this recipe with me.

...take of the best fruits in the land in your vessels,
and carry down the man a present, a little balm, and
a little honey, spices, and myrrh, nuts, and almonds...

GENESIS 43:11

*E*very Thanksgiving Mikey's elementary school held a canned food drive. He was very excited about it, and asked his mother what they could donate. He looked in the pantry, and was disappointed to find nothing of interest. There was just the usual stuff he didn't like to eat: canned green beans, peas, corn, and some chicken broth. He was spoiled, as his mother mostly cooked from scratch, using fresh ingredients. Even so, he was not a big fan of vegetables, fresh, canned, or frozen. "Can't you make them something good, Mom? Like your almondines?" Almondines were Mikey's favorite dessert—slivered almonds in a cookie-like crust drizzled with honey. He liked to do the honey drizzling himself. "Sure," his mother said, and they set about making pan after pan of almondines. They bought brightly colored tin cans at the store, and Mikey filled them with the homemade goodies. Now they do this every year, and Mikey delivers them to school. Of course his mother always puts one can aside for Mikey to eat when he comes home.

The next time you give to a food drive, make something special for those in need. Something unexpected—and truly appreciated.

ALMONDINES

This sweet dessert celebrates honey and almonds,
as good for you as The Bible says.

ENOUGH FOR 4 TO 6

1 refrigerated piecrust at room
temperature for 5–10 minutes

1¹/₂ sticks butter or margarine

1 cup (200 grams) sugar

¹/₂ teaspoon almond extract

1 cup (110 grams) slivered almonds

honey

DIRECTIONS: Unfold piecrust and place in greased pizza pan.
Combine butter and sugar and cook over medium heat until mixture
comes to boil. Boil for 1¹/₂ minutes. Add almond extract and slivered
almonds and stir together. Remove from heat. Pour over piecrust,
spreading mixture evenly. Bake at 375°F (190°C) for 15–20 minutes
or until golden. Drizzle with honey.

aunt susie's tips:

*Refrigerated piecrusts come with two in a box. You
may want to make both of them as these are pure
heaven and so easy. If the piecrust comes apart,
just pinch it back together. If you don't like the
taste of almond, use vanilla extract and replace
almonds with pecan or walnut pieces.*

...and that ye have good remembrance
of us always, desiring greatly to see us,
as we also to see you.

1 THESSALONIANS 3:6

When my granddaughter was around five years old, we were driving along in the car one day when she suddenly said to me, "I bet Grandpa's reckon to play with me." I looked at her with a puzzled expression and said, "What did you say?" She repeated to me excitedly, "I bet Grandpa's reckon to play with me." I still didn't know what she was talking about. I said to her, "What does that mean? What does 'reckon' mean?" She said to me, as if I should have known, "I bet Grandpa's reckon to play with me because every time I ask him if he wants to play with me, he says 'I reckon.'" I laughed about it afterward and remember that story fondly.

Memories provide a way for us to relive our past experiences. This ability to look back and remember allows us to appreciate that which God has given us.

PEACH DUMPLINGS

Through these peach dumplings I share wonderful memories of
my mother with my granddaughter. Make some for yours.

MAKES 8

SYRUP:
1½ cups (330 grams) brown sugar
¾ cup (180 milliliters) water
1 stick margarine or butter, melted
1 teaspoon flour

DUMPLINGS:
1 package refrigerated piecrusts (2)
1 16-ounce (450-gram) package
  frozen peach slices
Buttery spray
Cinnamon sugar

DIRECTIONS: Put brown sugar, water, margarine, and flour in a sauce-pan and bring to boil. Break each piecrust into four quarters for a total of eight. Place a couple of frozen peach slices on each quarter of piecrust. Spray peaches with buttery spray. Sprinkle peaches with ⅛ teaspoon cinnamon sugar. Bring corners of piecrust to center and pinch together, sealing peaches inside. Prick each dumpling with a fork. Place dumplings in a greased 9" × 13" pan. Pour syrup mixture over top of dumplings. Bake at 375°F (190°C) for 35–40 minutes until browned.

My sister Lois shared Mom's recipe with me.

aunt susie's tips:
*For those of you who like more syrup, increase the recipe by half.
If you have any extra peaches left, add them to the syrup.*

Brethren, be followers together of me,
and mark them which walk so as
ye have us for an ensample.

PHILIPPIANS 3:17

*C*hildren are very much influenced by what they see, and naturally often imitate these things. I remember when my granddaughter was around five years old. Her new favorite video was a cartoon called Lady Lovelylocks, who was the heroine of the show. The villainess, Raven Waves, was always threatening to cut off Lady's hair to take away her power. One day, my granddaughter came in with a pair of scissors she had gotten out of the drawer. She looked at me and said in her most threatening Raven Waves voice, "How about a haircut, Lady?" To my surprise, she had cut a few strands of her hair right to the nape of her neck. It was funny and enlightening at the same time. She was literally imitating the behavior she had seen on this cute show. When I look at the various shows on television in this day and age, I am very grateful that role models like Barney and Mr. Rogers are on the air to help shape our children's lives and behavior in a positive way.

Be a good role model for the children in your life. If you follow Christ's example, you can't go wrong.

SUGAR CREAM PIE

Baking a pie such as this is an old-fashioned way
to nurture children in a modern age.

SERVES 6 TO 8

———*✿✿✿*———

1 1/2 cups (300 grams) sugar

5 tablespoons flour

1 egg, separated

3 cups (710 milliliters) milk

1/2 stick butter or margarine

1 teaspoon vanilla

1 unbaked pie shell

Pinch of nutmeg

DIRECTIONS: Mix sugar and flour together in a saucepan. Add
egg yolk. Gradually mix in milk. Heat on stove and add butter, stirring
continuously until it thickens. Remove from heat. Add whipped egg
white and vanilla. Pour into unbaked pie shell and sprinkle with nutmeg.
Bake at 400°F (200°C) for 25 minutes.

My niece Marilyn shared this recipe with me.

*I was not in safety, neither had I rest,
neither was I quiet; yet trouble came.*

JOB 3:26

*E*ver have trouble getting your children to wear a seat belt?
I constantly had to remind my two daughters, Stacey and Joelle, to buckle up until . . . Stacey was seventeen and Joelle was eight when we went to California to visit my sister Marilyn. My sister Lois also went with us. Marilyn decided to take us on a ride through the streets of San Francisco. Lois was riding in front and the girls and I were in the back. We were going up and down the hills at a pretty fast pace and bouncing up and down in the backseat. Stacey frantically whispered in my ear, "Mom, she's going to kill us! Help me find my seat belt." Joelle whispered loudly in my other ear, "Mom! Make her slow down! Where's my seat belt?" We all quickly belted ourselves in, and I tried to calm the girls down. All of a sudden, as my sister came to a sudden stop, she hit my sister Lois in the chest with her right hand, knocking the breath out of her. She was trying to stop her from lunging forward, but she did it with too much vigor. We all survived and laughed about it many times. It certainly taught my children the value of a seat belt and the safety it can provide!

Safety can be an illusion, but it is always available when you are in God's hands. Turn to Him for safekeeping.

CHOCOLATE FONDUE

Chocolate fondue is always a safe choice
for a spectacular dessert.

SERVES 4

3 ounces (90 milliliters) heavy cream

3 1.55-ounce (45-gram) chocolate
bars

1 teaspoon rum extract or
brandy extract

DIRECTIONS: Heat heavy cream in a saucepan over medium heat.
Break chocolate bars into small pieces. Add chocolate pieces to heavy
cream and stir until blended together. Add rum or brandy extract. Pour
into serving bowl. Serve with chunks of angel food cake and fruit.

aunt susie's tips:
*If you have an electric fondue
pot, the chocolate fondue can be
prepared in the pot.*

*Be kindly affectioned one to another with
brotherly love; in honour preferring one another;*

ROMANS 12:10

How many times have you gone into a store only to have the salesperson or cashier be rude or unfriendly to you? I know it's happened to me too many times to count. In one particular case, I used to go to one of our local fast-food drive-through restaurants quite often. An older lady was usually working the window when I drove through. She was almost always very curt with me with nary a smile, but she would always give the obligatory, "Have a nice day." Well, I decided to make it one of my missions in life to be extra nice to her to see if she would ever respond in kind. About twice a week I visited the drive-through, trying to see if I could make her smile. After a month's time, she finally started smiling and being friendly to me.

A little kindness goes a long, long way. Ask God to help you emulate His kindness.

CHOCOLATE ALMOND PIE

A slice of this pie should sweeten the temperament of anyone feeling glum. Present one as a random act of baking kindness.

SERVES 6 TO 8

4 eggs

1 cup (235 milliliters) light corn syrup

1 cup (200 grams) sugar

2 tablespoons butter or margarine, melted

$^{1}/_{2}$ tablespoon flour

1 teaspoon vanilla

1 cup (170 grams) chocolate chips

1 cup (110 grams) slivered almonds

1 frozen prepared piecrust, thawed, unbaked

DIRECTIONS: Beat eggs, corn syrup, sugar, butter, and flour in a large bowl. Stir in vanilla. Add chocolate chips and almonds, stirring together. Pour into piecrust. Bake for 25–30 minutes at 350°F (180°C).

And to godliness brotherly kindness;
and to brotherly kindness charity.

2 PETER 1:7

O ne of the many benefits of running my own business was meeting so many different interesting and genuinely nice people. One of these people was a man named Jim, the owner of the laboratory where I first took my popcorn for calorie testing. He showed me around the lab and introduced me to the people who were working there. On one occasion I had to deliver a pie to him. It was the treat of the month, a gift given to him by his staff. He was on his way to a meeting and was in a bit of a hurry. I handed him the box with the pie inside, and he tilted it up a little bit, and the pie started leaking out of the box all over the front of his suit. I tried to help, but instead I made matters worse and got more pie on his suit. He couldn't have been nicer. He made a comment to the effect of how good the pie was. We got a wet cloth, spot cleaned his suit, and he was on his way. I was so thankful for the gracious manner in which this man handled my slipup.

Kindness is a virtue that informs our character. With God's help we can make the world a better place by being kind to one another.

SPLIT PIE

Brighten a lonely shut-in's summer evening with this fruity pie.

SERVES 6 TO 8

1 12-ounce (340-gram) container frozen whipped topping, thawed

1 cup (230 grams) sour cream

1 small box (3.4 ounces [100 grams]) instant vanilla pudding

1 9-inch prepared graham cracker crust

3 ripe bananas, sliced

1 small can crushed pineapple, drained well

1/2 dozen strawberries, sliced

1/2 cup (75 grams) blueberries, optional

1/2 cup (60 grams) chopped pecans

1/4 cup (30 grams) maraschino cherries

DIRECTIONS: Mix whipped topping, sour cream, and vanilla pudding together. Spread half of filling over crust. Add bananas, pineapple, strawberries, and blueberries. Spread remaining filling over fruit. Top with pecans and maraschino cherries. Refrigerate for 1–2 hours and serve.

My friend and neighbor April shared this recipe with me.

...thou shalt love thy neighbour as thyself...

LEVITICUS 19:18

*P*eople in many places don't even know the people who live next door to them. I am happy to say that we live in a neighborhood where many of us do know each other. We have a range of ages—young families, middle-aged families, and retired people. Our neighbors are kind, generous, giving people who are always willing to lend a hand to help each other. A couple of years ago, I decided to put in some pavers and plant a few bushes. I thought I could do it all on my own, but I quickly realized I was in over my head. Luckily, my neighbors, April and Jim, came to my rescue. Jim pulled out all of the bushes with a forklift while April and I ran to the garden center to buy new bushes. I wanted to have the new bushes in place before my husband, Larry, came home that evening. Talk about working fast! But with their help, we did it!

Friendly, tolerant, helpful neighbors make life so much more wonderful. They are just one more of the many blessings God has given us

BLUEBERRY PEACH COBBLER

Be a good neighbor. When someone new moves into your neighborhood, treat them to this delectable cobbler.

SERVES 8 TO 10

1 16-ounce (455-gram) package frozen peach slices

1 cup (155 grams) frozen blueberries

1 teaspoon baking powder

¼ teaspoon salt

1³/₄ cups (350 grams) sugar, divided

4 tablespoons margarine, melted

1 cup (125 grams) flour

¹/₂ cup (120 milliliters) milk

1 tablespoon cornstarch

1 cup (240 milliliters) boiling water

DIRECTIONS: Rinse frozen peaches and frozen blueberries with water and separate into individual pieces. They do not have to be thawed. Place the peaches and the blueberries on the bottom of a greased 11-inch pan. Mix the baking powder, salt, ³/₄ cup (150 grams) of the sugar, margarine, flour, and milk and pour over the peach and blueberry mixture. Mix 1 cup (200 grams) of the sugar and corn starch together, and sprinkle evenly over the batter. Pour boiling water over the top. Do not stir. Bake at 325°F (160°C) for 45 minutes to 1 hour or until top is golden brown. Let cool for 10 minutes.

My friend and neighbor April shared this recipe with me.

aunt susie's tips:
Very good served warm with ice cream. Also may be served cold.

If I laughed on them, they believed it not; and the light of my countenance they cast not down.

JOB 29:24

A smile, according to Webster's dictionary, is a favorable, pleasing, or agreeable appearance. Of course, the definition doesn't tell us how good a smile can make us feel or how good your smile can make others feel as well.

Not long ago, I was at my doctor's office, and this older woman was sitting across from me also waiting to see the doctor. She seemed rather down, so I started talking with her. Pretty soon we were having a good conversation. She had been having a really bad day; in fact, a really bad few months. Her only son had ended his own life a few months ago, and she was still greatly suffering from this loss. We talked for a while and also laughed a little bit. When the time came, we exchanged names so we could keep in touch with each other. She said our conversation had made her day as she smiled at me, and I in turn told her that she had made my day as well.

As they say, a smile is a frown turned upside down. God gives us much to smile about, so put that smile on and brighten someone's day.

CHOCOLATE CREAM PIE

Put a smile on someone's face with some of
this satisfying chocolate cream pie.

SERVES 6 TO 8

3 cups (710 milliliters) milk, divided

1 5-ounce (140-gram) package
cook-and-serve chocolate pudding

1 6-ounce (170-gram) prepared
chocolate crust

1 2.8-ounce (80-gram) package
raspberry chocolate mousse mix

1 8-ounce (230-gram) container
whipped topping

Shaved chocolate and chopped
nuts, optional

DIRECTIONS: Add 2 1/2 cups (600 milliliters) milk to pudding mix.
Cook pudding in microwave for 6–8 minutes, stirring at 2-minute inter-
vals. When pudding is thick, pour into prepared cookie crust. Place in
refrigerator until cool to set pudding. Prepare mousse mix using 1/2 cup
(120 milliliters) milk. Mix on high speed with an electric mixer for 2–3
minutes or until mixture thickens and changes color. Layer mixture on top
of the pie. Refrigerate until cool. Spread the thawed whipped topping on
pie. Decorate with shaved chocolate and nuts as desired.

My friend Judy shared this recipe with me.

The LORD killeth, and maketh alive: he bringeth down to the grave, and bringeth up.

1 SAMUEL 2:6

My father's death was very hard to accept, even though we knew he was dying of cancer. He lived for six months after the diagnosis of his illness and became just a shell of a man. My mother's death came less than five months after his and was even more devastating. The autopsy revealed that cancer had spread throughout her entire body. The fight to keep my father alive had kept her going. Then when he died, her strength was nearly gone. Before the autopsy was performed, they actually believed that she died of a broken heart. I was seventeen at the time and just could not deal with the death of my parents. In spite of having my sisters, I felt so alone. No matter what our age, the death of a loved one is hard for us to deal with, even as we know they are smiling down on us from heaven. Today, when I miss my folks, I make this recipe, a "quickie" version that recalls the angel food cake my mother used to make for my father, from scratch.

The passing of a loved one is a devastating loss. How can anyone get through it without our Lord's help? Don't hesitate to call Him in your time of need.

ANGEL FOOD CAKE WITH ICE CREAM

In times of sorrow, good food offers a welcome diversion.
Use this delicious cake to help lift a friend's spirits.

SERVES 6 TO 8

1 angel food cake

1 half gallon (1.9 liters) cherry cordial ice cream, softened

1 20-ounce (570-gram) can dark cherries

DIRECTIONS: Put cake on cake plate. Slice cake crosswise into three sections and separate layers. Spread first layer with ice cream. Put middle slice of cake on top of ice cream. Spread ice cream on second cake layer. Put top layer of cake on. Cover the entire cake with remaining ice cream. Freeze for one hour before serving. Cut into slices and spoon dark cherries over cake. Serve with chocolate sauce if you like.

My friend Shar shared this recipe with me.

aunt susie's tips:

Sherbet is good for this in the summer in place of the ice cream. You may buy a prepared angel food cake at your local grocery store.

For where your treasure is,
there will your heart be also.

MATTHEW 6:21

How many of you have been blessed with a sister-in-law who is a treasure beyond words? My husband's sister Gayle is our family treasure. Gayle and I used to go shopping together quite often when the children were younger. We shopped for clothes for the kids, did some birthday shopping, Christmas shopping, and "just for fun" shopping. On one such instance we were in a small men's clothing store in downtown Dayton, Ohio. We were looking at shirts, which were on this ten-foot clothes rack in the middle of the store. All of a sudden, I turned my ankle and started to fall. I quickly grabbed the clothes rack to try and stop my fall. Instead of stopping my fall, the clothes rack was leaning over as I fell to the floor. Luckily, Gayle had grabbed one end of the rack, and the sales clerk ran over and grabbed the other end of the rack. I was so embarrassed. Gayle took me to the urgent care office where they X-rayed me and gave me crutches, as I had broken my ankle. This is only one of the many, many times she has been there to help me. She has been a treasure to my family and me.

God puts people in our lives who are hidden treasures. Let these people know how much you value them.

Coffee Cake

Take this moist cake along the next time you have
a coffee klatsch with one of the treasures in your life.

Serves 8 to 10

1 cup (225 grams) butter or
margarine, softened

2 cups (400 grams) sugar

2 eggs

1 teaspoon vanilla

1 cup (230 grams) sour cream

2 cups (250 grams) flour

1 teaspoon baking powder

$^1/_2$ teaspoon salt

TOPPING:

$^1/_2$ cup (60 grams) nuts

1 teaspoon cinnamon

$^1/_2$ cup (110 grams) brown sugar

DIRECTIONS: Cream butter and sugar. Add egg and vanilla. Fold in
sour cream and add dry ingredients. Pour half of the batter into a greased
9" x 13" pan. Combine topping ingredients in a small bowl. Sprinkle half
of the topping over the batter. Pour the rest of the batter into the pan and
top with the rest of the topping. Bake at 350°F (180°C) for 40 minutes.

My friend and neighbor Celia shared this recipe with me.

aunt susie's tips:
*I double the amount of
topping as we like more of it
on our coffeecake.*

Enter into his gates with thanksgiving,
and into his courts with praise: be thankful
unto him, and bless his name.

PSALM 100:4

I was worried about our son when he had to have his tonsils removed. After the surgery, he was supposed to be in the hospital for two days. However, the doctor in charge of his care was leaving for vacation, and he dismissed our son after just one night in the hospital. I was a little concerned, but the doctor said he was doing fine. Against my better judgment, I brought him home. We had just gotten Tim settled on the sofa in the family room when he started feeling bad and spitting up blood. He had started hemorrhaging. We frantically picked him up, carried him to the car, and drove as fast as we could to the hospital. He was starting to pass out as we arrived at the emergency room entrance. I can't tell you how scared we all were. It took them over ten attempts to get an IV started. All we could do was pray and wait. After a while, they stabilized him, and the color started coming back to his cheeks. He ended up staying a week in the hospital and had a good recovery, perhaps quickened by my sneaking in this favorite cheesecake pie.

We never hesitate to turn to the Lord when a loved one becomes ill. Remember to thank God for your loved ones in times of health and sickness.

CHEESECAKE PIE

This yummy cheesecake pie will make anyone thankful.
Share some with an ailing friend.

SERVES 6 TO 8

1 8-ounce (230-gram) plus 1 3-ounce (85-gram) package cream cheese, softened

2 eggs

1/2 cup (100 grams) sugar

1/2 teaspoon vanilla

1 prepared graham cracker crust

TOPPING:

1–1 1/2 cups (230–345 grams) sour cream

6 tablespoons sugar

DIRECTIONS: Place cream cheese in a large mixing bowl, and beat until smooth. Add one egg at a time, beating well after adding each one. Gradually add sugar and vanilla, mixing well. Pour into graham cracker crust. Bake at 350°F (180°C) for 20 minutes. Prepare topping while the pie is in the oven. Blend sour cream with sugar. When pie is done, remove from oven. Spread topping on pie and return to oven for 2 minutes. Turn oven off, leaving pie in for additional 3 minutes. Remove, cool, and chill.

My sister Marilyn shared this recipe with me.

Finally, brethren, farewell. Be perfect, be of good comfort, be of one mind, live in peace; and the God of love and peace shall be with you.

2 CORINTHIANS 13:11

This past year I lost a very dear friend, Mary, who died at the young age of sixty-one from breast cancer. Mary was two years ahead of me in high school, but we were in some of the same clubs and became very good friends. We kept in touch off and on over the years. When Mary was about twenty-four, she married a widower with six young children and became an instant mom. She and her husband had four more children, making ten children in all. This amazing woman had a heart of gold, loved life, and loved her husband and their children. Mary had a full life and passed on her loving spirit to all who knew her. When I would talk to Mary on the phone (which wasn't often enough), we would reminisce and laugh a lot about old times. She would always tell me thanks for making her laugh. My one regret is that I didn't call Mary often enough, and I didn't get a chance to say good-bye to her and make her laugh one more time.

Old friends are the best friend. Call an old friend today—before it's too late.

Pineapple Nut Cake

Share a cup of tea and this old-fashioned cake
with an old friend today.

SERVES 10 TO 12

2 cups (400 grams) sugar

2 cups (250 grams) flour

2 teaspoons baking soda

1 teaspoon vanilla

2 eggs

1 20-ounce (570-gram) can crushed
pineapple

$^1/_2$ cup (60 grams) nuts

ICING:

1 8-ounce (230-gram) package
cream cheese, softened

1 stick margarine, softened

1 $^3/_4$ cups (210 grams) powdered
sugar

1 teaspoon vanilla

$^1/_2$ cup (60 grams) nuts

DIRECTIONS: Mix all ingredients together. Beat well for $1^1/_2$ –2
minutes. Bake in a greased 9" × 13" pan for 35–45 minutes at 350°F
(180°C). For icing, mix the cream cheese and margarine. Add remaining
ingredients and beat well. Spread icing over cake while the cake is still
warm. Refrigerate cake.

BREAKFAST, BEVERAGES & SAUCES

Then was our mouth filled with laughter,
and our tongue with singing…

PSALM 126:2

All kinds of funny stories happened at my popcorn and candy store. I may not have made much money, but it was an experience that I will never forget, and neither will a lot of other people. One day, a frequent customer came into our store. He had been overseas for about three months, and the first place he wanted to come to was our store. He wanted some of our "to die for" white chocolate almond popcorn. He was with a new girlfriend and wanted to impress her. I ran from the back of the store to the front part of the store to go and hug him, and I tripped over my own feet. As I was tripping, I grabbed his legs, pulling him down on top of me. At the same time I heard a big R-I-P, and my brand-spanking-new pants split open. Fortunately, neither one of us was hurt (my pride was certainly hurt, however), and we just started laughing. Of course, I had to cover up my bottom pretty quickly. His new girl was not quite sure what to make of us, but soon she joined in, too. Our laughing was quite contagious. We sent them both home with a free big bag of white chocolate almond popcorn, and they were very happy.

Happiness is being able to laugh at our mistakes and at ourselves. God loves a cheerful spirit. Be one.

GEORGIA'S TASTY MUSH

My friend Georgia spoils her loved ones with this
homemade mush and lots of good cheer.

SERVES 6

1 cup (140 grams) corn meal
1 cup (240 milliliters) cold water

3 cups (720 milliliters) boiling water

DIRECTIONS: Combine corn meal and cold water. Using a whisk,
slowly stir this mixture into 3 cups of boiling water. Lower the heat and
continue cooking for 15 more minutes until mixture is nice and thick.
Cook longer, if necessary. Pour into greased bread pan and refrigerate.
Slice and cook as desired.

My friend Georgia shared this recipe with me.

aunt susie's tips:
*I like to heat a slice in the
microwave and serve it with a
dab of butter and a sprinkle
of cinnamon sugar.*

Blessed are the peacemakers:
for they shall be called the children of God.

MATTHEW 5:9

*T*he role of the peacemaker isn't an easy one, and the world is full of peacemakers, but I think the biggest group has to be moms. When the children were little, it seemed that keeping peace in the home was a never-ending task. "Mom, he has my doll." "Mom, she knocked my Lincoln Logs down." Well, you know how it goes. On and on and on. Before I had children, I noticed how my nieces and nephews would constantly fight with each other. Little did I know mine wouldn't be any better. It seemed as though I needed a referee's uniform and a big whistle to maintain order and keep the peace. Would that it were as easy to keep the peace between some adults.

The role of peacemaker is many times a thankless job, but what a meaningful one. Ask God for the strength and patience to fulfill this role.

YUMMY BAKED PANCAKE

Kids won't squabble on a full stomach. If you need a little peace,
fill their little mouths with this mouth-watering pancake.

SERVES 4 TO 6

½ cup (120 milliliters) milk
½ cup (60 grams) flour
3 eggs
2–3 tablespoons butter

DIRECTIONS: Mix above ingredients, except butter. Melt 2–3
tablespoons butter in glass pie plate. Pour pancake mixture into pie
plate and bake at 400–425°F (200–220°C) for 15–20 minutes or until
lightly browned. Serve with jam of choice, pancake syrup, or butter and
powdered sugar.

My friend Sharon shared this recipe with me.

aunt susie's tips:
*I like to put lemon juice on top of
my butter and powdered sugar.*

And thou shalt have joy and gladness...

LUKE 1:14

Nothing creates joy like a snow day—no school! It was a Thursday, two weeks before Christmas, and all of the neighborhood children had come to our house and wanted to go sledding with our granddaughter. It was a beautiful snowfall—huge snowflakes out of a fairy tale that made everything look beautiful. The weather was perfect for sledding. It was a little cold, but they kept plenty warm with all the running around they were doing outside. They went sledding for about an hour, and then they decided that they needed to warm up, so in they came. It was time for fresh eggnog and chocolate chip cookies right from the oven. They were so full of joy. After refueling themselves, off they went again to sled and frolic in the snow. Right at that moment, God was looking over them and seeing that all was right in their world.

Little things in life can bring you joy and gladness in a big way. Ask God for deeper appreciation for the little joyful things in life.

CREAMY EGGNOG

Celebrate your next "snow day" with this thick and creamy eggnog. Grownups can add a bit of rum or whiskey.

SERVES 8

6 eggs
6 tablespoons sugar
1 quart (580 grams) vanilla ice cream, softened
1 quart (1 liter) milk

DIRECTIONS: In a large bowl, beat 6 eggs until fluffy. Add sugar 1 tablespoon at a time. Gradually mix in ice cream, slowly adding milk. Serve immediately.

aunt susie's tips:
You can serve this with nutmeg or cinnamon, and try using some brandy or rum extract.

*I have fought a good fight, I have finished
my course, I have kept the faith…*

2 TIMOTHY 4:7

My husband enjoys telling the story of his grandfather and the bumblebees. As a young farm lad, he and his grandfather started painting an old tool shed on a hot summer day. Suspended on ladders with their paintbrushes in hand, they noticed to their chagrin that they had disturbed a nest of bumblebees. In a split second, my husband abandoned the ladder and expected Grandpa to follow suit. But Grandpa—not one to retreat from a few flying pests—remained on the ladder and started swinging at the bees with the only thing he had available: a short board. Bees diving in for the kill, and Grandpa, clutching to his ladder with one hand and swinging his board with the other. Bumblebee air power dominated over human board-swinging power; Grandpa was forced to retreat from the ladder with more than a dozen stings to his credit. Rather than being welcomed home as the fallen, brave warrior, Grandpa was received with an "Are you nuts?" reaction by Grandma. The stinging was so severe that Grandpa was rubbed with a home-remedy paste of baking soda and water and sent to bed. Two days later, Grandpa and my husband returned to the tool shed with appropriate battlefield gear: protective clothing and a gallon of chemical spray. During the second round of battle, the bumblebees met their match.

The lesson of this story? Like St. Paul, you should be ready to "fight the good fight" but depend on God to help you choose the right battles.

HONEY BUTTER

Celebrate life's little victories with a cup of tea
and toast spread thick with this sweet honey butter.

MAKES ABOUT 2½–3 CUPS

1 pound butter (450 grams), softened
1 14-ounce (400-gram) can condensed milk
1 tablespoon honey

DIRECTIONS: Cream butter in a large bowl. Beat in condensed milk and whip until fluffy. Add honey, blending well.

My friend Shar shared this recipe with me.

aunt susie's tips:
*I divide this into four parts and
keep refrigerated. Try this—you
won't believe how good it is!*

That which is gone out of thy lips thou shalt keep and perform; even a freewill offering, according as thou hast vowed unto the LORD thy God, which thou hast promised with thy mouth.

DEUTERONOMY 23:23

Most children try things they are not supposed to at least a few times during their childhood, and I wasn't any exception. When we were in the eighth grade, a friend of mine brought a package of her mother's cigarettes to my house. We were having a slumber party and were going to watch a movie on our brand-new television. Oh, were we excited. While it was still light, we hiked to the nearby woods, and all of us girls decided to try to smoke a cigarette and be just like the grown-ups. Well, I puffed and puffed and started coughing and couldn't quit coughing, and so did most of the girls. I couldn't see why people liked these things so much. When we left, somehow the cigarettes were put in my purse. Well, the next morning after the girls had gone, my mother wanted to talk to me. It seemed she had found the cigarettes in my purse and was very upset and, even worse, disappointed with me. She told me how much it would hurt my father if he found out that I had done this. She told me that if I promised not to do this anymore, this would be just between the two of us. I kept my promise.

Remember how important God's promises are to you. That's how much your word means to others—so keep your promises.

BAKED FRENCH TOAST

A good breakfast is a promise we should all keep to ourselves and our loved ones. Promise them French toast for breakfast, and they'll wake up bright and early.

SERVES 6 TO 8

12 slices Italian bread

8 eggs

2 cups (480 milliliters) milk

2 teaspoons rum extract

³/₄ cup (170 grams) butter or margarine, melted

1¹/₃ cups (300 grams) brown sugar

3 tablespoons light corn syrup

1 cup (95 grams) sliced almonds

DIRECTIONS: Place bread slices flat on the bottom of a greased 9" × 13" baking dish. In a large bowl, beat eggs, milk, and rum extract. Pour mixture over bread. In mixing bowl, blend melted butter, brown sugar, and corn syrup until smooth. Spread over bread. Sprinkle with almonds. Bake uncovered at 350°F (180°C) for 1 hour or until golden brown.

My friend Kathi shared this recipe with me.

aunt susie's tips:
You can make this ahead of time and refrigerate overnight before baking.

Then Sarah denied, saying, I laughed not;
for she was afraid. And he said, Nay;
but thou didst laugh.

GENESIS 18:15

How many of you have laughed when you shouldn't have? When living with my sister and her husband, Paul, we lived in a tri-level home, and Paul would always tell me to stop running on the stairs or I was going to break my neck. One afternoon my sister called for Paul. She yelled up the stairs for him, and pretty soon he came running down the hall and down the stairs, not heeding his own advice. As fate would have it, he came tumbling down the last two stairs and landed with a big thud. As I watched this happen, I tried not to laugh, but I could not contain myself. I started laughing uncontrollably as Paul winced with pain. Luckily, my brother-in-law has a good sense of humor and had a laugh about it later. My sister and I helped him to his feet and to the doctor. It turns out he had broken his tailbone. After finding that out, I felt terrible. I didn't know that he had been seriously hurt. Paul recuperated fast and never lets me forget how hard I laughed when he was so miserable.

You ever laugh when you shouldn't have? Sometimes laughter helps ease our pain. Call on God when you find times hard to bear.

PICANTE SAUCE

Gather some friends together for some love and laughter
while you munch on chips and this party favorite.

MAKES ABOUT 4 CUPS

1 28-ounce (800-gram) can diced
   tomatoes, drained

1 4.5-ounce (135-gram) can chopped
   green chilies

2 jalapeño peppers, diced

2 scallions, sliced

2 teaspoons lime juice

1 tablespoon sugar

$1/2$ teaspoon garlic salt

DIRECTIONS: Mix ingredients in blender on low. Increase jalapeños
for spicier sauce. Best served with lime-flavored tortilla chips.

My friend Phil shared this recipe with me.

Thou art welcome, daughter.
God be blessed, which hath brought thee unto us.

TOBIT 11:17

One of the most understanding people I have ever known is a former high school teacher of mine, Sister Kathryn Ann. When I was in high school, I often went through hard times, especially when my parents died, and Sister Kathryn Ann was always there to console me. She would meet with me at least once a week after school just to talk, and it helped me immensely. Sister Kathryn Ann is now retired and lives about fifteen miles from my home. She usually calls me several times a year and always remembers to send me Christmas cards and birthday cards. I, on the other hand, have not taken the time to keep in touch with her on a regular basis. I always seem to have good intentions, but I invariably get waylaid. The last time I went to visit her, she made me feel so welcome, and we picked up right where we had left off the last time we had seen each other. She is a wonderful friend who loves me, flaws and all, and for that I am deeply grateful.

Sometimes we take our most understanding friends for granted. Ask God to help us remember to thank these special people.

PINEAPPLE SAUCE

The pineapple is a symbol of welcome; whip up this fondue sauce and welcome a neglected friend today.

MAKES ABOUT 1 CUP

—◊◊◊—

$^3/_4$ cup (240 grams) pineapple preserves

2 tablespoons prepared mustard

1 tablespoon horseradish

DIRECTIONS: Mix all ingredients in saucepan and heat for 2–3 minutes. Serve with beef or chicken fondue.

And let the peace of God rule in your hearts,
to the which also ye are called in one body;
and be ye thankful.

COLOSSIANS 3:15

*I*n my college years, due to my irresponsible attitude, I was not doing well in school at Purdue University. As my parents had died a few years earlier, my eldest sister, Anita, was my guardian, along with the aid of my other two sisters. They were very displeased with my progress at school. We all met for a discussion of my future plans. They insisted that I either move in with my sister Marilyn and her family and attend an all-girls college in Cincinnati or quit college and get a job and support myself. I made the choice to live with my sister Marilyn, her husband, Paul, and their young daughter Paula and continue my education. I was miserable at first, as this meant leaving the town where I grew up and leaving all of my friends behind. I was under the close supervision of my sister and her husband, "the Captain." (Her husband was in the Army.) Although I cried and cried, my tears never moved the Captain. He never would indulge me, and in time my attitude improved, and I came to love my new home in Cincinnati. I am very thankful for their strong, positive influence on my life.

Give thanks to God for those people in your life who love you so much that they do what's best for you, even when you don't much like it.

Sweet and Sour Sauce

Life is sweet and sour, as are the best of friends
and this sweet and sour sauce.

MAKES ABOUT 1 CUP

—⁂—

1/2 cup (120 milliliters) cider vinegar

1/2 cup (120 milliliters) chicken broth

1/2 cup (110 grams) packed brown sugar

1 tablespoon cornstarch

2 tablespoons water

DIRECTIONS: Combine cider vinegar, chicken broth, and brown
sugar in a saucepan and bring to a boil. Combine cornstarch with water
in a small cup, stirring until smooth. Slowly add cornstarch/water mixture
to saucepan until desired consistency is reached. Sauce will thicken as
it cools.

A generous man will prosper;
he who refreshes others will himself be refreshed.

PROVERBS 11:25 NIV

When my partner and I expanded our business and moved from our little store (it was only 400 square feet) to a larger (1,200 square feet) one, we needed a loan in order to do so. As we had been in business for only a year and were not yet making a profit, the banks did not want to help us. My good friend, Mary, introduced us to her friend, Ralph, a dear gentleman who was willing to help us find an investor. Talk about a prayer being answered. He introduced us to Randy, who ran a foundry business of his own in Ohio. Our meeting with him went well, and even though he had never met either one of us before this meeting, he was willing to take a risk and give us the loan we needed. He has always had a generous spirit and a big heart. Thanks to him, we were able to move to a local shopping center and start expanding our store. We still stay in touch.

Friends are constantly sharing their generosity with us, as is the Lord our God. Be generous with others as they are generous with you.

CRANBERRY RELISH

Don't wait for Thanksgiving to provide a feast for the people who help you most. Serve this cranberry relish with turkey or pork.

MAKES ABOUT 2 CUPS

1 16-ounce (450-gram) can whole-berry cranberry sauce

¼ cup (80 grams) orange marmalade

½ cup chopped walnuts

½ can mandarin oranges, drained and diced

DIRECTIONS: Pour cranberry sauce into bowl. Add marmalade and nuts, stirring in oranges. Mix thoroughly. Refrigerate until serving.

My friend Judy shared this with me.

aunt susie's tips:
I add sugar to taste, as I like mine a little sweeter.

...it is the gift of God...

EPHESIANS 2:8

*A*s the baby of our family, so much younger than my sisters, I really didn't have a close relationship with my sisters after they left home. I felt like I was an only child and didn't fully realize how much of a gift from God they were. After my youngest sister got married and left home at the age of nineteen, it was just Mom, Dad, and me. After my parents' death, though, my sisters became my parental figures, my support system, and my guardians. As a result, I developed a closer relationship with each of them. Today my sisters and I make it a priority to keep in touch with each other and get together at least once a year—all four of us—as we don't live very close to each other. We've gotten lost in downtown Boston, had pillow fights in motel rooms, and nearly got kicked out of one of the restaurants we were in because we were laughing so loudly. The relationship that I have with my sisters is very dear to me. It is a rare gift, for which I am grateful.

Praise God for the gift of your sisters, brothers, uncles, aunts, etc.

—⟨∾∾∾⟩—

GRITS WITH CHEESE

Breakfast is our first opportunity each day to
break bread—or these yummy grits!—with our
loved ones. Be sure to say a blessing.

SERVES 4 TO 6

4 cups (1 liter) water

1 cup (245 grams) quick-cooking grits

1/2 cup (115 grams) butter or margarine

1 cup (240 milliliters) milk

1/2 teaspoon minced garlic

1/2 cup (60 grams) shredded
cheddar cheese

4 eggs, beaten

DIRECTIONS: Bring water to boil. Gradually stir in grits. Cook for 3–5
minutes, stirring occasionally. Remove from heat and add remaining ingredients. Put into a greased 8" × 8" baking dish. Bake at 350°F (180°C) for
45 minutes to 1 hour.

My sister Anita shared this recipe with me.

aunt susie's tips:

*If you want to add a little tang to
this, try using a dash of hot sauce.
Also, it would be good with pepperjack cheese for a pretty hot taste.*

... Be strong and of a good courage; be not afraid, neither be thou dismayed: for the LORD thy God is with thee whithersoever thou goest.

JOSHUA 1:9

Hospitals and surgical operations instill fear in many people. When our youngest daughter, Joelle, needed to have her tonsils removed at age ten, she was terrified at the prospect. As the date of the operation gradually approached, she counted off the days and hours to her forthcoming "doom." Once situated in her room and wearing her hospital gown before the tonsillectomy, her imagination started to run wild. She was sure that her last hours were here, and that she would not return alive from the operation. Despite our efforts to calm and reason with her, Joelle believed that the end was near. When the hospital staff arrived with the gurney to transport Joelle to the operating room, her fears took over. On the way out of the room, Joelle extended her arms and grabbed on to the doorframe, preventing the gurney from being pushed through the doorway. They had to pry her arms from the door as she screamed and cried for me. It was a heart-wrenching sight, especially for a mother. As expected, the operation was successful. To Joelle's amazement, she was alive, with a very sore throat. To this day, we remember Joelle clinging to the doorframe with all her might, and we have a good laugh.

Fear, however irrational, is a serious thing, and we need to comfort family members, friends, and even strangers in their hour of need.

EGGY CHEESE CASSEROLE

Food is comfort and love. Comfort someone you love with a
helping of this casserole, which is good any time day or night.

SERVES 8 TO 10

1 stick butter or margarine

$1/2$ cup (60 grams) flour

9 large eggs

1 cup (240 milliliters) milk

1 3-ounce (85-gram) package cream
cheese, softened

2 cups (450 grams) cottage cheese

$1/2$ pound (230 grams) shredded
Monterey Jack cheese

$1/2$ pound (230 grams) shredded
pepperjack cheese

1 teaspoon baking powder

1 4.5-ounce (130-gram) can chopped
green chilies

DIRECTIONS: In medium saucepan, melt butter and stir in flour. Add
eggs and milk, stirring until well blended. Stir in cream cheese and cottage
cheese until smooth. Mix in Monterey Jack, pepperjack, baking powder,
and chilies. Pour into a greased 9" × 13" pan. Bake uncovered at 350°F
(180°C) for 45 minutes.

My friends Kathi and Bev shared this recipe with me.

ACKNOWLEDGMENTS

—◦◦◦—

There are so many people who helped make this book possible. I am very grateful to each and every one of them for their contribution and assistance. Thanks goes to all those at Rockport Publishers. They include Ken Fund, Holly Schmidt, Paula Munier, Dalyn Miller, Brigid Carroll, Wendy Simard, Janelle Randazza, Claire MacMaster, and Sandy Smith. With their time consuming endeavors, this book gets whipped into shape and ready to go to press. My daughter Stacey was invaluable, working with me many long hours to complete this. My husband Larry also lent a hand when needed and helped contribute to this book. My daughter, Joelle, and my sisters always were encouraging me. I also want to thank April, Kathi, and Sharnell for all of their help in cooking and tasting the wonderful recipes included here. I especially want to thank all of you who gave me such wonderful recipes. Unfortunately, I could not use all of the recipes I received, but I am very thankful to everyone who took the time to give me his or her favorite recipe. I adapted some of these recipes to accommodate the 10-minute format of this book. This book would not have been possible without all of you. Thanks for your wonderful gift of friendship. I would also like to thank my many friends and relatives who were not mentioned in this book, as you were all of great inspiration to me.

INDEX